THE
CRUCIBLE
OF
DOUBT

THE
CRUCIBLE
OF
DOUBT

**REFLECTIONS ON THE
QUEST FOR FAITH**

TERRYL GIVENS
FIONA GIVENS

DESERET
BOOK

Salt Lake City, Utah

Library of Congress Cataloging-in-Publication Data

Givens, Terryl, author.
    The crucible of doubt : reflections on the quest for faith / Terryl Givens, Fiona Givens.
        pages cm
    Includes bibliographical references and index.
    ISBN 978-1-60907-942-0 (hardbound : alk. paper)
1. Faith. 2. Church of Jesus Christ of Latter-day Saints—Doctrines. 3. Mormon Church—Doctrines. I. Givens, Fiona, author. II. Title.
    BX8635.3.G57 2014
    234'.23—dc23   2014019187

Printed in the United States of America
Publishers Printing, Salt Lake City, UT

10   9   8   7   6   5   4   3   2   1

TO ZINA AND BOYD

Disciples of the God who laughs

It is not like a child that I believe in Christ and profess faith in Him, but rather, my *hosanna* has come through the great *crucible of doubt*.

—Fyodor Dostoevsky[1]

•———————•

Crucible, *n*. [LL. *crucubulum,* a hanging lamp, an earthen pot for melting metals]

A vessel used for melting or refining substances which require a strong degree of heat, as metals, ores, etc.

CONTENTS

CONTENTS

PARADIGMS AND PREMISES:

STARTING OFF ON THE WRONG FOOT

•————•

In the area known as the Netherbow, located along the Royal Mile in Edinburgh, Scotland, there is a magnificent restored house, built shortly before Columbus sailed for the New World. It is called the John Knox house, but that great reformer lived in it only briefly, if at all. The house was actually occupied in the sixteenth century by James Mossman, goldsmith to Mary, Queen of Scots. Mossman was, as one might expect, a man of great wealth. He was also a brilliant craftsman and artificer. On the third floor of his substantial home is a room protected by a heavy oak door. Off center, on the right of a large iron panel that conceals the locking mechanism, is a keyhole.

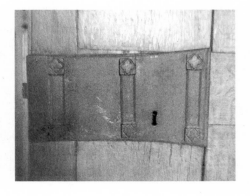

It does not appear to be a lock that would be more resistant than most to tampering or picking, but it is. No burglar, no matter how

1

ingenious, ever did or ever could gain access to the room by manipulating the mechanism accessed through this keyhole. No skeleton key—no, not even the master key itself—will turn the heavy tumblers and open the lock that guards the room. At least, not via this keyhole.

For the keyhole is a dummy keyhole. The ornamental bar next to it conceals the real keyhole and the location of the true lock.

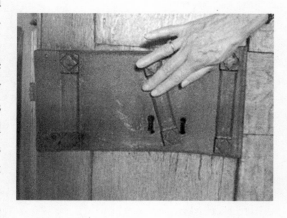

It is impossible to know how many would-be thieves dulled their picks and rubbed their fingers raw in a fruitless effort to gain access to the riches on the far side of Mossman's door. Their assumption would have been reasonable enough: Here is the door, here is the keyhole, this is the way to the treasure. But their assumption would have been wrong.

We all inhabit geographical, linguistic, and social worlds that shape our vision and our impressions of what is normal, what is real. Our worldview is a collective set of assumptions we carry with us that condition every question we ask. These "paradigms" make it possible to guide inquiry, but they can also limit and impede our inquiry. They can get us off on the wrong foot, obscure our line of sight, or simply misdirect our focus. This is because, all too often, we don't realize the limiting assumptions with which we are working.

We can't easily step outside most such preconceptions. Even recognizing the extent of our unexamined assumptions can be the hardest thing of all. It is like asking a fish what it is like to be wet. "What is wet?" even a miraculously verbal fish would reply. Our assumptions, like the ocean in which a fish swims, are the invisible background to our thinking, waking existence. Only when we have left a misguided assumption behind are we able to see it clearly. Then we no longer ask why ships do not fall off the edge of the world. We don't bind women we don't like, throw them into a pond, and watch to see if they float or sink. Neither do scientists try to measure the earth's motion relative to the space through which it speeds. Flat earths, witchcraft, and the cosmic ether are no longer part of our intellectual universe. We now see them for the erroneous frameworks they were. They have gone the way of alchemy and philosophers' stones. It should not be that difficult to recognize the implications of these transformations for our present circumstances and lives; we are inevitably living under the burden of some paradigms, individually and collectively, that will one day be relics with other conceptual assumptions we have cast off. It is only with hindsight that we can see the paradigms of the past for the intellectual straitjackets they were.

The important point, however, is that those frameworks are not just themselves error-laden. Erroneous assumptions do not just forestall truth and progress, although that would be cause enough to lament their malign influence in our lives. They are like the dummy lock of Mossman's home. They point us in the wrong direction, limit our understanding, and even warp the questions we ask. Worse, they create the conditions for faulty reasoning and disastrous conclusions. In past ages, bad paradigms led well-intentioned physicians to bleed to the brink of death and beyond millions of the already sick and enfeebled. No scientist had reason to seek for the sources of disease in filth, fleas, or dirty water in a world where the four humors were believed to govern all physical and emotional health.

In the realm of religion and spirituality, as in the areas of science, medicine, and public order, wrong assumptions can provide invisible deterrents to a life of religious devotion. Such flawed paradigms have been known to trouble even stalwarts of the faith. Great

Christian thinkers of the past have operated with assumptions—some of them deeply ingrained, sanctioned by long tradition, by ecclesiastical authority, and by scripture—that made answers difficult or impossible to obtain. At the least, such assumptions can delay prayerful responses to earnest questions, even by decades.

One such example involved one of the greatest mystics of the Middle Ages. Julian of Norwich was a model of piety. Living in England's second-largest city in a time of rampant plagues, she fell gravely ill in her thirtieth year. As her sickness reached a crisis in 1373, she experienced a series of heavenly visions. She recovered her health and retreated into solitude in order to meditate upon the sixteen revelations, or "showings," she had received. Catholics, Anglicans, Lutherans, and others revere her today as a holy woman, a faithful disciple of the Gentle God. It is impossible to read Julian and not be profoundly affected by a version of the Father's love that has rarely been expressed so vividly and movingly and convincingly. In reading her, one is immersed in the experience of Divine Love.

Julian spent the next twenty years in voluntary seclusion, continuing to ponder and reflect upon the outpouring of light she had experienced in order to determine its full meaning. As she struggled to reconcile her visions with the religious tradition in which she had been raised, a few questions in particular came into urgent focus. For the sake of clarity and inner resolution, she asked God (1) to show her hell and purgatory and (2) to explain the nature of sin. Isolated from all distractions, she spent her days in fasting and study and prayer. Months became years, and still no illumination came. After two decades, the light at last broke through the darkness. Twenty years it took for her to escape the confines of her preconceptions and realize the answers were delayed because her questions were wrong.

Raised a severe Catholic, Julian had been taught that sin was a cosmic catastrophe and a damnable defect in each human heart. Hell, she had learned, was the fitting fate of the depraved sinner, and purgatory a nether world of punishment in which the penitent anxiously awaited their redemption. But that was a view wholly out of keeping with the nature of the God who had manifested Himself in her visions. This God now revealed to her that the hell and purgatory expounded in her faith tradition did not exist. As for sin, she learned that there is "no harder hell than sin."[1] Hell was not a fixed place of retribution, but the experience of our own alienation from God. In other words, hell is the condition of suffering that results from sin.

Here, too, Julian was schooled in a radical reconstruction of her assumptions. "I thought if sin had not been," she wrote, "we should all have been clean and like unto our Lord as he made us." He could have, He should have prevented our sinning, she reasoned. "For then, I thought, all should have been well." To her surprise, she learned through the parable of the Lord and His servant (in her Revelation 14) that "sin is behovely," or necessary.[2] God's mercy and Christ's Atonement can make sin an occasion for "profytable" learning rather than "dyspeyer."[3]

In Latter-day Saint culture, many stumble over the declarative tone of "Be ye therefore perfect" (Matthew 5:48). Two considerations soften the command: First, the wording in 3 Nephi 12:48 is different—and in an important way. "I would that ye should be perfect," Christ implores, in what sounds like gentle beckoning to join Him rather than a daunting order across infinite distance. Second, Joseph Smith loved Luther's translation of the Bible, in which the word usually rendered *perfect* (*teleioi*) is rendered as *vollkommen*, that is, *complete, whole, entire*. The Atonement is not a backup plan in case we happen to fall short in the process; it is the ordained means whereby we gradually become complete and whole, in a sin-strewn process of sanctification through which our Father patiently guides us.

Humans courageously venture forth into mortality, Julian was taught, and as they experience sin and error, they learn to cleave to the virtuous and holy ("they taste the bitter, that they may know to prize the good").[4] From God's perspective, sin is a vital, necessary component of the learning process of life that He, as master gardener, will prune and forgive. It is not a damnable malice on our part that elicits God's anger. Sin, along with the pain it entails, is the great educator. Mortality is the school in which we learn to eschew evil and to inculcate the attributes of the Divine. It is instructive, in this regard, that it was *after* Eve and Adam had eaten the fruit in the garden that God said, "Behold, [they have] become as one of us, to know good and evil."[5]

What we learn from Julian's experience is that clarity and enlightenment often require that we first relinquish our paradigms, no matter how dearly held. Julian's twenty-year quest to see the lakes of fire and brimstone and fathom the mystery of human depravity could unfold no faster than she was willing to let go of her premises. That can be a wrenching process, requiring much time—and much humility.

In the modern Church too, stalwarts have sometimes found their operating frameworks an impediment rather than an aid to faith, as the example of B. H. Roberts demonstrates. From his first experience debating a Campbellite minister on the Book of Mormon in 1881, Roberts was devoted to defending the Mormon scripture. While in England as a Church mission president in 1887 and 1888, he studied in the Picton Library, collecting notes on American archaeology that could serve as external evidence in support of the Book of Mormon. The three volumes of the work that resulted, *New Witnesses for God*, appeared in 1895, 1909, and 1911. Then on August 22, 1921, a young member wrote a letter to Elder James E. Talmage, a member of the Quorum of the Twelve Apostles, that would shake up the world of Mormon apologetics and dramatically refocus Roberts's own intellectual engagement with Mormonism.

The brief letter sounded routine enough. "Dear Dr. Talmage," wrote W. E. Riter, one "Mr. Couch [a friend of Riter's] of Washington, D.C., has been studying the Book of Mormon and submits the enclosed questions concerning his studies. Would you kindly answer them and send them to me."[6] Talmage forwarded the five questions to the Church's Book of Mormon expert, B. H. Roberts, expecting a quick and routine reply. Most of the questions dealt with anachronisms that one could explain as near-equivalents employed by the translator. But one that had Roberts stumped was this question: "How [are we] to explain the immense diversity of Indian languages, if all are supposed to be relatively recent descendants of Lamanite origin?" To put the problem in simple terms, how, in the space of a mere thousand years or so, could the Hebrew of Lehi's tribe have fragmented and morphed into every one of the hundreds of Indian languages of the Western Hemisphere, from Inuit to Iroquois to Shoshone to Patagonian. Languages just don't mutate and multiply that quickly.

Several weeks after Talmage's request, Roberts still had not responded. In late December, he wrote the President of the Church, explaining the delay and asking for more time: "While knowing that some parts of my [previous] treatment of Book of Mormon problems . . . had not been altogether as convincing as I would like to have seen them, I still believed that reasonable explanations could be made that would keep us in advantageous possession of the field. As I proceeded with my recent investigations, however, and more especially in the, to me, new field of language problems, I found the difficulties more serious than I had thought; and the more I investigated the more difficult I found the formulation of an answer to Mr. Couch's inquiries to be."[7]

Roberts never found an answer to that question, and it troubled him the rest of his life. But here is the lesson to be learned from this story. Roberts's dilemma was born of a particular view he held about the occupants of the New World. He believed that Lehi arrived on an empty continent, and that his descendants and his descendants alone eventually overran the hemisphere from the Arctic Circle to the Straits of Magellan. If that had been the case, then the language problem—along with a good many others—is indeed insoluble. Everything from the DNA of all Native Americans to several hundred languages spoken throughout the pre-Columbian hemisphere to a New World panoply of cultural artifacts would have to point to one and only one point of origin: a small, Hebrew-speaking colony over two millennia ago.

However, the actual text of the Book of Mormon does not require that we read Lehi as entering upon an uninhabited continent. In fact, the record itself contains the materials to read a very different context behind the Lehite settlement. As early as Jacob 7, that record keeper mentions one Sherem "who came among the people of Nephi." And this stranger, apparently unexpectedly, "had a perfect knowledge of the language of the people."[8] One would hardly trouble to mention that someone spoke perfect Hebrew if he were from a Hebrew-speaking background. The reasonable inference that follows from this, in other words, is that Sherem came from an indigenous people or a different group of settlers than the Nephites. And his was unlikely to have been the only non-Nephite or non-Lamanite group.

In fact, there are alternative points of view about the geography of the Book of Mormon, including the notable work of John Sorenson, who has examined the record's seven hundred references to geography and constructed a self-consistent map with an area of Nephite and Lamanite habitation some five hundred miles long and perhaps two hundred miles wide (or about the size of Palestine).[9] And though as late as 1981 the Book of Mormon introduction referred to Lamanites as "the principal ancestors of the American Indians," nothing in that book of scripture necessitates such a claim. That is why, as of 2007, the Church changed the wording to "the Lamanites are among the ancestors . . ." In other words, more recent critical thinking about the Book of Mormon has resulted in the recognition that its geographical scope may be much narrower and its cast of characters much broader than most Mormons were accustomed to believe. The Book of Mormon itself permits the reasonable inference that Lehi's colony represented one of any number of migrations by sea and by land bridge. His descendants, according to readings of the text now prevalent, likely occupied a relatively small region and intermingled and intermarried with other peoples and cultures over succeeding generations. Roberts couldn't figure out how Inuit and Patagonian languages derived from Hebrew for a simple reason: they probably didn't. And there was no necessity to try to make that square peg fit into that round hole. It was like trying to make the tumblers turn in the James Mossman door. The faulty question itself had no answer any more than Mossman's dummy keyhole had a key.

Daniel Dennett wrote, "Philosophy . . . is what you have to do until you figure out what questions you should have been asking in the first place."[10] Disciples too must persevere until we get the questions right. If a devout visionary and an ordained Seventy can ask the wrong questions, it is likely that many of us do as well. We are all prisoners of our preconceptions and faulty models. Those are frequently the problem in faith crises—not the questions that arise from them. After all, the Restoration unfolded because a young man asked questions. The scriptures are replete with encouragement to question—"ask that you may know the mysteries of God" is a common injunction, as is the oft-quoted verse from James 1—"If any of you lack wisdom, let him ask of God, that giveth to all . . . liberally . . . ; and it shall be given"—and we also receive many assurances that questioning will bear fruit: "surely shall you receive a knowledge of whatsoever things you shall ask in faith."[11] The unexamined paradigms with which we begin can negatively affect a healthy propensity to question. They can point us in the wrong direction, misdirect our attention, or constrain the answers we are capable of hearing. In those circumstances, as Joseph Smith learned, some people "will fly to pieces like glass as soon as anything comes that is contrary to their traditions."[12]

Various faulty conceptual frameworks, or paradigmatic pathogens, may undermine our spiritual immune systems and create an environment where the search for truth becomes all search and no truth, where we find ourselves "ever learning, and never able to come to the knowledge of the truth."[13] To be open to truth, we must invest in the effort to free ourselves from our own conditioning and expectations. This means we have to pursue any earnest investigation by asking what the philosopher Hans Georg Gadamer calls the "genuine question." And that is a question that involves openness and risk. As he explains, "our own prejudice is properly brought into play by being put at risk."[14] With the faith that is open to any answer, we can never be sure what we will learn next. As the seed of faith sprouts and grows, we cannot know how the branches will bend or where the roots will twist. The genuine question yields results we could seldom anticipate—if we can but find a vantage point where the spiritual chambers of our soul are sufficiently still and the mental terrain is adequately clear. Claustrophobic assumptions extend far beyond the supposed geography of hell or of the Nephites. In what follows, we will reexamine a number of paradigms that may make the quest for faith and the path of discipleship more painful and tortuous than it need be.

CHAPTER 1

OF METHOD AND MAPS:

THE USE AND ABUSE OF REASON

·——•——·

O WORLD, thou choosest not the better part!
It is not wisdom to be only wise,
And on the inward vision close the eyes,
But it is wisdom to believe the heart.
Columbus found a world, and had no chart,
Save one that faith deciphered in the skies;
To trust the soul's invincible surmise
Was all his science and his only art.
Our knowledge is a torch of smoky pine
That lights the pathway but one step ahead
Across a void of mystery and dread.
Bid, then, the tender light of faith to shine
By which alone the mortal heart is led
Unto the thinking of the thought divine.

—GEORGE SANTAYANA[1]

Then beneath the color there was the shape. She could see it all so clearly, so commandingly, when she looked: it was when she took her brush in hand that the whole thing changed. It was in that moment's flight between the picture and the canvas that the demons set on her who often brought her to the verge of tears and made this passage from conception to work as dreadful as any down a dark passage for a child. Such she often felt herself—struggling against terrific odds to maintain her courage; to say: "But this is what I see; this is what I see," and so to clasp some miserable remnant of her vision to her breast, which a thousand forces did their best to pluck from her.[2]

We know more than we think. And we know in more ways than we sometimes realize because different ways of knowing abound. The call of the beautiful, the vision granted by love, and the voice of conscience are merely three examples. All give us glimpses of realities not otherwise available to us. The poet and the artist anciently had something approaching a sacred status in the world. The Greeks so revered the literary arts that Sophocles was chosen to be a leader of Athens purely on the strength of his success as a playwright.[3] The Greeks sensed that the best art does not take us away from reality into the dreamy realms of fantasy—though some may do that. On the contrary, the best art penetrates the hard shell of habit to reimmerse us in the depths of experience, "refining the sense of beauty to agony," " making the stone more stony," creating "anew the universe, after it has been annihilated in our minds by the recurrence of impressions blunted by reiteration."[4] A Mozart or a Milton, like a Moses or the Psalmist, approximates a reality we sense is true, though prophets and artists alike struggle to capture in language just what it is that has been unfolded to their vision. Like

13

Virginia Woolf's Lily Briscoe in the passage above, who can intuit but not capture the truth before her, we want to get to the bottom of it all, to make sense of a life far too nuanced and complex to capture with a simple brushstroke. William Wordsworth spent the greater portion of his life wrestling with one question in particular: how do blood and bones, friends and family, childhood terrors and early loves, a favorite toy and the ghosts of past melodies, all come together and blend into a coherent self, an "I"?

> *Dust as we are, the immortal spirit grows*
> *Like harmony in music; there is a dark*
> *Inscrutable workmanship that reconciles*
> *Discordant elements, makes them cling together*
> *In one society. How strange, that all*
> *The terrors, pains, and early miseries,*
> *Regrets, vexations, lassitudes interfused*
> *Within my mind, should e'er have borne a part,*
> *And that a needful part, in making up*
> *The calm existence that is mine when I*
> *Am worthy of myself!*[5]

Like Wordsworth's poem itself, art becomes a vehicle not just for describing life but for interpreting life, revealing its hidden patterns and purposes. The quest for, and recognition of, what is beautiful—is that not a search for knowledge and understanding of the highest kind? Do we not have a sense, in the presence of Beethoven's Ninth Symphony, or Michelangelo's *David*, or Van Gogh's *Starry Night*, that we have arrived at something that is neither instrument nor pastime but an end perfect in itself? Great art takes us to a place where we realize the need for another kind of language to capture the deepest realities. Watching a performance of *Othello* tells us more about how the worm of jealousy can be insinuated into a man's heart and destroy his marriage than any psychology textbook could. *Uncle Tom's Cabin* did more to inflame a society against the evils of slavery than any cost-benefit analysis of the Southern economy could. Picasso's *Guernica* is a more powerful indictment of the horrors of war than the most carefully compiled tables of statistics. And Charles Dickens did more to animate Christians against the evils of child exploitation and institutional brutality than any government report by experts.

Another way of saying this is to note that Albert Einstein's breakthroughs made Hiroshima possible. John Hersey's book of that title convinces us why Hiroshima must never happen again. None of this is because art merely entertains us or indulges our imagination. And it is certainly not because art takes emotion out of the picture so we can judge and act with prudent objectivity. On the contrary—the best art gives human emotion its due. In each of the examples mentioned, the artist's depiction of human emotion, informed by moral conscience, is shown to be one of the greatest mechanisms in civilization's arsenal against the evils of this or any time.

Can any claim be more specious than to suggest that we want more objectivity, and less emotion, in guiding the course of our personal and collective lives? Emotion is not a defect in an otherwise perfect reasoning machine. Reason, unfettered from human feeling, has led to as many horrors as any crusader's zeal. What use is pity in a world devoted to maximizing efficiency and productivity? Scientific husbandry tells us to weed out the sick, the infirm, the weak. The ruthless efficiency of euthanasia initiatives and ethnic cleansing are but the programmatic application of Nietzsche's point: from any quantifiable cost-benefit analysis, the principles of animal husbandry should apply to the human race. Charles Darwin himself acknowledged that strict obedience to "hard reason" rather than sympathy for fellow humans would represent a sacrifice of "the noblest part of our nature."[6] It is the human heart resonating with empathy, not the logical brain attuned to the mathematics of efficiency, that revolts at cruelty and inhumanity.

In Byron's great tragedy *Cain*, Lucifer convinces the title character that for the teeming miserable of the world, the calculus of human suffering suggests it were better never to have been born. When Cain expresses his agreement in the presence of his sleeping child, his terrified wife snatches the baby to protect him from where her husband's frightful logic seems to lead. "Why so fearful?" a bewildered and hurt Cain asks his wife. "I would not accost the sleeping infant with anything ruder than a father's kiss."[7] For it is with the eyes of a father, not of a cold calculator, that even the ill-starred Cain beholds his son.

In most of life's greatest transactions, where the stakes are the highest, it is to the heart that we rightly turn, although not in utter isolation from the rational and reasonable. But whom to marry, when to discipline a child, when to let go of a dream, what sacrifices to make and promises to keep—these are decisions best made when emotion is moderated but not obliterated by reason, by logic, by "scientific" thinking. And these decisions are certainly made, not in the absence of truth, but in recognizing those very truths which logic and science may be powerless to detect.

To take one of the most important instances of this fact, we may look to the insight of the philosopher William Luijpen. Luijpen points out that "we must consider *love* as an attitude by means of which certain aspects of reality become visible. The true meaning of the other as other, i.e., the meaning of the other as subject, becomes visible only through love. An attitude of preoccupation with ourselves, with our own desires and interests, precludes our access to the true meaning of the other."[8] This is not just metaphoric language. In the most emphatic and urgent meaning of the word, love *reveals* truth. It does not create the impression of truth; love does not merely endow something with a subjective truth—love is the only position or emotional disposition from which we become fully aware of the already present reality of the other person as more than a mere object among other objects in a crowded universe. Love

16

alone reveals the full reality and value of the other person. We have all known the experience of waiting at a crowded intersection for the traffic to clear. Vehicles and their drivers meld into simple impediments, things, impersonal obstacles to *our* purposes. Common sense reveals that farther down the road, I myself become one such simple, soulless interruption to some other weary traveler. But my mind revolts at the notion that to other drivers, as to the earth's teeming billions, I am a thing, a nuisance, a paltry digit in an almost infinite sequence of numbers, an "it" rather than an "I."

The same violent jolt to my sense of self occurs when I enter a store and see myself on the closed-circuit monitor. An icy, awkward moment of unease. I stare in quasi-unbelief. It is not the simple response to an appearance that disappoints or surprises me. It runs deeper. It is my dismay at the utter inadequacy of the representation. For there I am, appearing to all the world as an object, an externality, a mere shape with opaque surfaces and outsides. But my experience of myself is radically different—radically fuller, more expansive, interesting, complete. My *self* as I experience it is inseparable from my past, my memories, my experiences, my thoughts, my love of Cadbury's chocolate and my dislike of Adam Sandler movies. I know that this self, the one I live as and through, with an interior world as big as the cosmos, is the real self, not that collection of atoms passing across the monitor. You may ask, but what am I *objectively?* Is not such a qualifier misleading? Do a camera, a DNA sequencer, and a full-spectrum lab report provide the truest, the richest account of *who I am?* Or do my spouse, my children, and my circle of friends? Love does not blur the reality behind the appearance. Love reveals reality. So why would we privilege scientific rationality *over* our intuitive, emotion-laden ways of perceiving truth? As the philosopher Hans Georg Gadamer argued, "Bracketing out human meanings from human science means understanding nothing at all."[9]

One form that love takes is a grateful heart. Gratitude itself is a conduit to the True. "Thanking," wrote Julian of Norwich, "is a true inward knowing."[10] The Mormon scholar Philip Barlow writes:

> My grateful mental state lets in a different view of reality than is otherwise possible. . . . And when I am thus conscious of my life and the world as a gift, I am less preoccupied with self. My attention focuses elsewhere. I am more alert to other people's needs and virtues. I find my wonder awakened by just about everything: the engineering behind the physique of a cricket or a fly, for instance, or the beauty in even a pebble. In other words, when I am grateful, I tend toward a higher mental (and spiritual) state. I take things— people, order, air, roundness, everything—less for granted. Hence I notice things otherwise invisible to me. It is as if I have a sixth sense, taking in more context, more reality. If my temporary taste of gratitude becomes a disciplined habit, an ongoing attitude and state of mind, I am "smarter," more aware, than if this were not so. To the extent that I become a habitually grateful person, I engage a different and richer reality than the "me" who is less grateful.[11]

Science can tell us a great deal about the world. It can tell us what the stars are made of, explain how a lightning bug flashes in the night sky, and describe the process of cell division that leads a zygote to become a baby girl. But it does not tell us why we should care about the nature of stars, why the staccato flash of insects in the night delights us, or how the child should live. The error of believing that science represents the highest, or purest, or only reliable guide to truth is the error of scientism. Philosophers like Maurice Merleau-Ponty have pointed out that the problem is not science itself, one of the greatest and most fruitful of all human enterprises. The healthy stance is not "to question the validity of physical laws or the veracity of mathematical equations, but rather . . . to break the dictatorship and absolutism of scientific thought over all other forms of human thinking."[12] This is perhaps why many of science's most brilliant figures, past and present, are critics of the supposed conflict between science and religion and are themselves perfectly comfortable espousing religious belief. As Freeman Dyson, one of the world's most esteemed theoretical physicists, explains, "Science is a particular bunch of tools that have been conspicuously successful for understanding and manipulating the material universe. Religion is another bunch of tools, giving us hints of a mental spiritual universe that transcends the material universe."[13] Contrary to prevalent myth, a recent, large study revealed that, in the U.S. at least, "scientists are only a bit less religious than the average American."[14]

The problem is not that science *cannot* give us direction with life's most urgent questions. It is because, in actual practice, logical reasoning *does not* give us much guidance. We don't really live our lives, in any meaningful way, according to the dictates of logic. And we certainly don't embrace our most cherished beliefs, values, or opinions on the basis of reason alone—however much we may protest we do. This was a point made by the great eighteenth-century philosopher David Hume. In explaining why two reasonable people can so seldom cross the divide of religious or political or intellectual difference, he provided this unsettling but profoundly powerful insight: "As reasoning is not the source, whence either disputant derives his tenets; it is in vain to expect, that any logic, *which speaks not to the affections*, will ever engage him to embrace sounder principles."[15] Hume made of this insight a principle that seems most unphilosophical: "Reason is, *and ought only to be* the slave of the passions, and can never pretend to any other office than to serve and obey them."[16]

Such a statement is easily taken out of context and ridiculed. But Hume's point was simply this: as moral agents, immersed in a world of human relationships and human values, we most appropriately choose and judge and act *as* human beings whose desires and motivations and bases for action are deeper than and prior to logic. For example, we read of an instance of child abuse—and if we are revolted by such an act of cruelty, it is because it elicits our *sense* of injustice, our *sympathy* with the victim, our *feeling* that something wrong has transpired. If we apply our reason to make sense of the event, it is to forge an argument for what we already *know* to be true. If we find we are unable to express that truth in the language of science, or to find logical support for our moral position, that should not blind us to the reality, the truth, that child abuse is wrong. In such a case as this, our failure to find support in science, or logic, or rationality, or whatever name we want to give it, should not cause us to *doubt* our intuitive moral faculty. On the contrary, it should cause us to place greater trust in and value upon it. Conscience has preserved us in our humanity, even if other ways of knowing have not.

The point in all these examples is this: the human impulse toward the sublime and the artist's revelation of the beautiful; love's power to unlock the full splendor of the other, its blinding revelation of the infinite worth of the individual; and conscience, with its unwavering response to moral imperatives, its piercing protest against evil and gentle enticement to recognize the good—all these are living proofs that different ways of knowing exist. We employ them, we rely upon them, and we trust in them. As well we should. The Astronomer Royal of Great Britain has recently written about one of astronomy's most puzzling and astonishing mysteries: dark matter. Apparently, the majority of the physical universe consists of material that science has not yet been able to detect. The *large* majority. As Martin Rees admits, "it's embarrassing that more than ninety per cent of the universe remains unaccounted for. Even worse," he continues, when we realize that the source of this undetectable bulk of our universe may reside in entities that are subatomic, or bodies millions of times more massive than our sun. The portion we can see and measure is miniscule: "The atoms that comprise our bodies and that make all visible stars and galaxies are mere trace-constituents of a universe whose large-scale structure is controlled by some quite different (and invisible) substance." We can hardly speculate as amateurs on where current astrophysical investigations might lead. But we hear the ring of truth and relevant wisdom in Rees's conclusion: what we can "see, as it were, [is] just the white foam on the wave-crests, not the massive waves themselves."[17] If we wish to penetrate those massive waves that constitute the ebb and flow of eternity, we will need all our resources, including those of art, of our moral sense, and of love.

CHAPTER 2

ON PROVOCATION AND PEACE:

OF LIFE'S FUNDAMENTAL INCOMPLETENESS

> *"Faith" is a fine invention*
> *When Gentlemen can see—*
> *But Microscopes are prudent*
> *In an Emergency.*
>
> —EMILY DICKINSON[1]

I n the last chapter it was suggested that we know more than we think; it is at the same time true that we know less than we want. People have a horror of loose ends. We crave closure and certainty, wholeness and equilibrium. We will watch a bad movie to its pitiful end rather than leave ourselves in suspense as to its conclusion. We may be more traumatized by a child gone missing than by one who meets a tragic end. The devout dream of an end to all anxious striving is captured in the universal hope etched on countless tombstones that we may at last "rest in peace." William Blake, the great English poet, captured the essence of childhood yearning and satisfying fulfillment in one of his most famous lyrics:

> *Little Lamb, who made thee?*
> *Dost thou know who made thee?*
> *Gave thee life, and bid thee feed*
> *By the stream and o'er the mead;*
> *Gave thee clothing of delight*
> *Softest clothing, woolly, bright;*

Gave thee such a tender voice
Making all the vales rejoice?
Little Lamb, who made thee?
Dost thou know who made thee?

Little Lamb, I'll tell thee
Little Lamb, I'll tell thee:
He is called by thy name
For he calls himself a Lamb
He is meek, and he is mild;
He became a little child
I a child, and thou a lamb
We are called by his name
Little Lamb, God bless thee!
Little Lamb, God bless thee![3]

Call and response, question and answer, yearning and fulfillment. In the rhythm of this "Song of Innocence," we see epitomized
the childhood vision of a world with no loose ends, no dark corners,
no lonely echoes. Blake contrasted this happy state with the fretful
terror of questions asked but unanswered in a sister poem, from a
collection he called "Songs of Experience."

Tiger! Tiger! burning bright
In the forest of the night
What immortal hand or eye
Could frame thy fearful symmetry?

In what distant deeps or skies
Burnt the fire of thine eyes?
On what wings dare he aspire?
What the hand dare seize the fire?

And what shoulder, and what art,
Could twist the sinews of thy heart?

26

And when thy heart began to beat,
What dread hand? and what dread feet?

What the hammer? what the chain?
In what furnace was thy brain?
What the anvil? what dread grasp
Dare its deadly terrors clasp?

When the stars threw down their spears,
And watered heaven with their tears,
Did he smile his work to see?
Did he who made the lamb make thee?

Tiger! Tiger! burning bright
In the forests of the night,
What immortal hand or eye
Dare frame thy fearful symmetry?[4]

The dropped beat at the end of each line is like a breath caught in mid utterance. Fears are raised but unresolved, tension grows, and, at the end, anxiety has been intensified rather than dispelled. That rude awakening, Blake is saying, goes hand in hand with our step into adulthood and the world of lived experience, a world where the circle closes all too rarely.

Like children, we adults also want our most pressing questions answered, not multiplied. So it is not surprising that we look to religion, the great comforter, to "resolve [us] of all ambiguities," in the words of Dr. Faustus.[5] But perhaps providing conclusive answers to all our questions is not the point of true religion.

Jesus, on assorted occasions, chided His listeners for just such misconceptions. The gospel Christ taught was spectacularly designed to unsettle and disturb, not lull into pleasant serenity. What's this? He asks. You thought you were doing well to not kill, not commit adultery? I am here to say you must examine yourself and go beyond conduct to search out your innermost motives and desires.

("Ye have heard . . . But I say unto you . . .") You went to the wilderness thinking you would find a soft-spoken prophet teaching nice pleasantries? John was something else altogether, wasn't he? ("What went ye out for to see?") You want to be my disciples? Do you think you have the slightest notion of the cost? ("Ye know not what ye ask. Are ye able to drink of the cup that I shall drink of?") You assumed my gospel would be about harmony and accord? Living my gospel will create intensely painful choices. ("I am come to set a man at variance against his father.") Peter writes epistles to the scattered Saints. But he does not write to console or comfort. Twice, he tells them, he writes "to stir up" his audience.[6]

These and numerous other episodes drive home the recurrent point that incitement, not equilibrium, is part and parcel of true religion. As Elder Jeffrey Holland said, the Savior did not preach "comfortable doctrine, easy on the ear." Rather, he upset the expectations of "those who thought he spoke only soothing platitudes."[7]

In the perfect peace of Eden, God planted a certain tree, the purpose of which was clearly provocation, not restful shade from the sun. From this first fruit placed to incite moral ambiguity and conflict, to the shocking dilemma Jesus forced upon a young would-be disciple to choose between honoring the dead or following the Savior, to Christ's enigmatic words about bringing not peace but a sword, Christianity is inseparable from provocation.[8] These thoroughly unanticipated turns of events, these shattering disclosures of wrenching conflict where peace and wholeness had been looked for, find their poignant culmination in John, chapter 6. Jesus has been teaching more difficult doctrines, more unsettling precepts that alienate and offend rather than console and invite. He is addressing not strangers or anonymous crowds but His own followers. And yet, we read, "Many therefore of his disciples, when they had heard this, said, This is an hard saying; who can hear it?" And "From that time many of his disciples went back, and walked no more with him."

Then, a Jesus wearied by the defections of fair-weather disciples asks His closest friends, "Will ye also go away?"[9]

Their answer is instructive. We usually read it as powerful affirmation of the apostles' faith, but between the lines is a more nuanced response. "To whom shall we go?" they ask. There is pathos in the unspoken. They do not say, "of course not, we have found all the answers right here," because Christ's words do not elicit peace but perplexity; they leave His apostles unsettled as well. The apostles do not say, "Why would we leave?" They do not reply by affirming their testimony of the difficult doctrines that have caused the fainthearted to flee. They are just as shaken as the others by what they have heard. They affirm their faith in Jesus *in spite of*, not *because of*, the hardness of the way, the disequilibrium His indecipherable teachings have stirred in their souls. The apostles choose to cling to the belief they have that Jesus is the Christ. But that doesn't make His teachings easier to bear.

Christ was Himself the Prince of Peace, and He promised peace to His followers. And that serene confidence in His promise is a comfort we are bidden to seek. But in light of the overwhelming conditions of tension and turmoil through which we wade, and the life of ever greater striving to which He calls us, it would seem this peace comes as strains of harmony heard amid the cacophony of life, like the quiet voice heard amidst the maelstrom of wind. It does not come as escape from the whirlwind.

The story of the garden and humankind's fall from grace is the foundational story of the Judeo-Christian tradition. Genesis is largely a book of etiologies, that is, a collection of stories that explain how things got to be the way they are. The flood explains the rainbow, the Tower of Babel the diversity of languages, God's rest on the seventh day the Sabbath. But the master etiology, the story that explains the human condition itself—the tale that answers life's most agonizing questions about pain and suffering and undeserved struggle—is the story in Genesis, chapter 3, which the

Christian world calls the Fall. Mormonism interprets that story in a way that is radically different from the perspective of the rest of Christendom. Yet even Mormons all too seldom arrive at the real meaning of the story, which is correspondingly out of sync with the Christian understanding of life's purpose. The traditional reading of Adam's and Eve's transgression is that it is the etiology for a life of toil, the pains of childbirth (and child rearing), our alienation from God, and life in a vast vale of tears. In Adam's Fall, we sinned all, as the colonial hornbook summarizes the story. Given the choice of good or evil, Eve—then Adam—chooses evil, and the retribution continues to unfold centuries later. Life is assumed to be about the fundamental, clear-cut choice between Good and Evil.

Mormonism sees no such simple dichotomy in the primeval options. Yes, obedience and safety and security in God's presence are presented as one of the choices. But Mormonism is more sympathetic to Eve's perception of the alternative: the beauty of the fruit, its goodness as food, its desirability "to make one wise." Not coincidentally, ancient philosophers like Plato considered that triad of ideas—Beauty, Goodness, Truth—to be the highest manifestation of divine virtue. In the Mormon narrative, therefore, the circumstances that define the reality of the human predicament are not a blatant choice between Good and Evil but a wrenching decision to be made between competing sets of Good. The philosopher Hegel believed that this scenario, replicated in myriad artistic narratives, expressed the inescapably tragic nature of the universe. There are very few simple choices. No blueprint gives us easy answers. Life's most wrenching choices are not between right and wrong but between competing demands on our time, our resources, our love and loyalty.

When Mormon pioneer Levi Savage's fellow Saints determined to pursue their ill-advised handcart venture too late in the summer, he foresaw disaster. But the only choices available to him were prudence and wisdom and self-preservation on the one hand, or solidarity and faithfulness to his friends on the other. Two incompatible Goods beckoned to him. And when two sets of Good compete, one is obliterated in the process of choosing. According to one witness, Savage said, "Seeing you are to go forward, I will go with you, will help you all I can, will work with you, and if necessary, will die with you; but you are going too late."[10] Savage chose loyalty, and he found horrific suffering. That is the tragic consequence. Eve founded the project of human mortality—and lost Eden.

That is why true religion is inseparable from suffering. It tells us the truth about our condition without flinching, offers no cheap solutions, and conceals none of the costly price. And the price that exacts the most from us is not the final, definitive resolution of the arena or the operating room. It is the fretsome anxiety of the waiting room. "There is no pain so awful as the pain of suspense," said Joseph Smith.[11] That is why we will do almost anything to escape this suspense. We feel unmoored if our religion fails to answer all our questions, if it does not resolve our anxious fears, if it does not tie up all loose ends. We want a script, and we find we stand before a blank canvas. We expect a road map, and we find we have only a compass. We have yet to learn, as the poet John Ciardi wrote, that "clean white paper, waiting under a pen, is a gift beyond history and hurt and heaven."[12] It is curious, in this regard, that so many critics attribute to religion a kind of facile wish fulfillment, imaginative fairy-tale scenarios that reduce complexity and mystery to easy answers and glib forms of consolation. As any disciple knows who has lived a life of faith thoughtfully, attuned to the rhythms of humanity's travails, to the demands of mercy and unconditional love, and to the call to patient waiting, religion is not the coward's way out of life's difficulties. As Flannery O'Connor wrote, "Religion costs. They think faith is a big electric blanket, when of course it's a cross."[13]

Christ's invitation to "take up [one's] cross, and follow" Him hardly sounds like a summons to serenity.[14] As Elder Holland has said, "Sadly enough . . . it is a characteristic of our age, that if people want any gods at all, they want them to be gods who do not demand much: comfortable, smooth gods."[15]

In considering the divinely appointed contrast between things that act and things that are acted upon,[16] it may be worth considering that freedom and its opposite take many forms. Freedom to choose belief and a life of faith, freedom to choose one's principles and abide by them, freedom to cherish one set of values over another, those kinds of freedom might best unfold when we are not commanded in all things, by God or by the facts. To be an agent unto oneself may very well require that we operate in the valley of incertitude. It is here that we act most authentically, calling upon intuition, spiritual intimations, or simple yearning. In this regard, William James observed that "our passional nature not only lawfully may, but must, decide an option between propositions, whenever it is a genuine option that cannot by its nature be decided on intellectual grounds."[17]

Perhaps we would do better if we came to understand the fundamental incompleteness of the blueprint as something other than a defect, a failure. It is the way it must be, and the way it should be. As the Catholic philosopher Michael Novak has suggested, we might consider, in the face of our unsettling reality, that "He desired a world of indetermination, with all its crisscrossing confusion, so that within it freedom could spread out its wings, experiment, and find its own way."[18] The grand project in which we are engaged is one that moves us *away* from stasis, ease, comfort, and equilibrium, and toward an end that is yet to be determined—precisely because our choices are yet to be made. "It doth not yet appear what we shall be."[19]

The indeterminacy of it all can be frightening—and disconcerting to those hoping for clear answers and neat solutions. Like the still-evolving universe, our lives and natures don't have prefabricated final versions. Even with Christ as our exemplar, we strive to achieve emulation, not replication. Brigham Young said it most provocatively: "'I put into you intelligence,' saith the Lord, 'that you may know how to govern and control yourselves.'"[20] If spiritual maturity and not a rote performance is the goal, then life is not a multiple-choice test. There *can't* be ready answers to the most soul-stretching dilemmas. Like Eve's courageous choice in the garden, the test has to probe deeper than True/False or Right/Wrong. Self-revelation and self-formation take place only in the presence of the seemingly insoluble, the wrenchingly vexing, the genuine question. Dennis Rasmussen calls that "the Lord's Question": "Into man's spiritual shell God places His question like a grain of sand. And man's work, daily renewed, is to make of it a pearl of great price."[21] Young described the principle more prosaically, but just as emphatically, when he described the gospel—and presumably the Church itself—as a system designed to be a provocative moral mirror in which we see our own shortcomings and weaknesses so we can amend them: "The gospel . . . causes men and women to reveal that which would have slept in their dispositions until they dropped into their graves. The plan by which the Lord leads this people makes them reveal their thoughts and intents, and brings out every trait of disposition lurking in their [beings]."[22] Such self-revelation is a painful—but ultimately healing—process.

This perspective represents a fundamental reorientation in attitude toward life's incompleteness. The patterns of meaning only dimly perceived, the inspiration only partially (or negligibly) felt, may not be God's indifference after all—or our spiritual failing. It may be the most potent form of the question most worth posing: What will you do now?

That question can be daunting, discouraging. Or it can be liberating. William Wordsworth found it empowering and worthy of celebration. Mormons know the early stanzas from his famous ode on immortality, the "trailing clouds of glory" lines, about birth as "a sleep and a forgetting," and our premortal abode in heaven.[23]

However, a good part of the grandeur of the poem is in its recognition that the poet's explanations are tentative leaps into the dark, not definitive solutions to life's mystery. Even premortal existence, Wordsworth told an interviewer, "is far too shadowy a notion to be recommended."[24] That is why he called his ode "*Intimations* of Immortality." That is what makes his poem all the more remarkable, and all the more a powerful endorsement of the orientation that celebrates the incompleteness of life. For this, Wordsworth's greatest poem, is an elaborate hymn of self-consolation. His lifelong preoccupation was with the gradual, inexorable decline of childhood faith and joy. It is the paradox of Eden: Eve and Adam only know what paradise is when they leave it. The garden to which they long to return only emerges in its full splendor from the distant plains of this dreary world. In a similar way, Wordsworth describes the typical child as one who "liest in Abraham's bosom all the year; and worship'st at the Temple's inner shrine," even though the child "know[s] it not."[25] Childhood is most valued and loved by those who have left it behind.

This is why Wordsworth's solution to his plight is a triumph of the moral imagination. He does not retreat into nostalgia for the simpler world of Blake's "Little Lamb," or into self-pity. He does not mourn the day long past, when all the pieces used to fit together, when life was a beautiful spectacle that brimmed with its own plenitude of meaning, when being fully alive to each new morning was reason enough to be happy. After struggling with the indelible sadness of adulthood, trying in vain to recapture the innocence and joy of childhood delight and spontaneity, Wordsworth realizes it is the tension itself, the irresolution, the ambiguity and perplexity of our lives, the very feelings of alienation, estrangement, and dislocation, that are our rescue from the complacency and stasis of an eternal Eden. Like the sand in the oyster shell, the torment of uncertainty is at the same time the spur to our spiritual vitality and growth. That is why, as he tells us, in the final analysis he appreciates the very things that plague the questing mind. He is grateful, he writes, *not* for the blithe certainties and freedom of a past childhood. He is thankful *not* for what we would expect him to appreciate,

> *not indeed*
> *For that which is most worthy to be blest—*
> *Delight and liberty, the simple creed*
> *Of Childhood, whether busy or at rest,*
> *With new-fledged hope still fluttering in his breast:—*
> *Not for these I raise*
> *The song of thanks and praise;*
> *But for those obstinate questionings*
> *Of sense and outward things,*
> *Fallings from us, vanishings;*
> *Blank misgivings of a Creature*
> *Moving about in worlds not realised, . . .*
> *Those shadowy recollections,*
> *Which, be they what they may,*
> *Are yet the fountain light of all our day.*[26]

It is in the midst of his perplexity, of his obstinate questions, uncertainties, misgivings, and shadowy recollections that almost, but don't quite, pierce the veil, that he finds the prompt, the agitation, the catalyst that spurs him from complacency to insight, from generic pleasures to revelatory illumination, from being a thing acted upon to being an actor in the shaping of his own spiritual identity. Similarly, it was unrest and spiritual agitation that kept Julian searching through twenty years of solitary contemplation.

The best models we can fashion, even aided and abetted by Restoration doctrines, leave lingering questions and points of disjunction and conflict. The process of deciphering the entirety is ongoing: "It will take a long time after the grave to understand the whole," said Joseph Smith.[27] But it is crucial to remember that cognitive dissonance lives on both sides of the faith divide, with believers and nonbelievers alike. A godless universe is hardly immune to the assaults on our mental equilibrium. Even cutting-edge quantum theory, according to one of its most famous proponents, "describes Nature as absurd from the point of view of common sense."[28] There is no escaping our fragmentary grasp on the deepest truths of our predicament, on either side of faith. In the memorable words attributed to the arch-skeptic Voltaire, "To believe in God is impossible; but not to believe is absurd."

To the would-be believer, not everything makes sense. Not all loose ends are tied up; not every question finds its answer. Latter-day Saint history can be perplexing, some parts of its theology leave even the devout wondering, and not all prayers find answers. Still, many of us believe the disciples had it right. "To whom [else] shall we go?"[29] The doctrines Christ propounded were troubling, challenging, and they apparently produced in that instance more provocation than peace, perhaps more cognitive dissonance than resolution.

Staying the course takes a great effort of will. Relinquishing faith would solve some problems—but would multiply others. For how does one even begin to address the manifold experiences and tender feelings we have known, the powerful ideas and explanations our theology provides, and the visitations of peace and serenity that are balm to broken hearts like our own? Abandoning our faith because it doesn't answer all the questions would be like closing the shutters because we can't see the entire mountain. We know in part, Paul said, looking for the flickering flame to give us a glimpse of the way ahead in the gloom. With Nephi, we readily confess: "I know that [God] loveth his children; nevertheless, I do not know the meaning of all things."[30] We know more than we think, even if we know less than we would like.

CHAPTER 3

OF SADDUCEES AND SACRAMENTS:

THE ROLE AND FUNCTION OF THE CHURCH

— • —

Nuns fret not at their convent's narrow room;
And hermits are contented with their cells;
And students with their pensive citadels;
Maids at the wheel, the weaver at his loom,
Sit blithe and happy; bees that soar for bloom,
High as the highest Peak of Furness-fells,
Will murmur by the hour in foxglove bells:
In truth the prison, unto which we doom
Ourselves, no prison is: and hence for me,
In sundry moods, 'twas pastime to be bound
Within the Sonnet's scanty plot of ground;
Pleased if some Souls (for such there needs must be)
Who have felt the weight of too much liberty,
Should find brief solace there, as I have found.

—WILLIAM WORDSWORTH[1]

Saints are nothing without a community of memory. . . .
To be a communion of saints makes saints possible.[2]

I t has been said that Jesus invented true religion, and man invented churches. That's not exactly right, but it does reflect a crucial principle: true religion is a way of life; a church is an institution designed to strengthen people in the exercise of that life. The English historian Thomas Carlyle defined a person's religion as the set of values evident in his or her actions, regardless of what the individual would claim to believe when asked. ("Holiness is right action," more simply.)[3] Our behavior is always oriented around a goal, a set of desires and aspirations, even if we are not always fully aware of them—or willing to own them. "A man's religion is the chief fact with regard to him," said Carlyle. "By religion I do not mean here the church-creed which he professes, the articles of faith which he will sign. . . . We see men of all kinds of professed creeds attain to almost all degrees of worth or worthlessness under each or any of them. . . . But the thing a man does practically believe (and this is often enough *without* asserting it even to himself, much less to others); the thing a man does practically lay to heart, concerning his vital relations to this mysterious Universe, and his duty and destiny there, that is in all cases the primary thing for him, and creatively determines all the rest. That is his *religion*."[4]

James defined religion more economically: "Pure religion and undefiled before God and the Father is this, To visit the fatherless and widows in their affliction."[5] It is worth considering what he meant by this, in light of Carlyle's insight. He could have meant that the best religious practice is to serve others. But perhaps more accurately, one could take his words to mean this: a life devoted to serving others reflects the best conceivable set of values. Regardless of what we *say* we believe, such a life *shows* what we believe: that our hearts are attuned to others, that we feel the pain of the vulnerable and seek to relieve it, that we aspire to emulate Christ and His life of selfless service. If that kind of compassion—the act of putting ourselves in the place of the other and seeking *his or her* best interest—is the lodestar of our life, then *that* is true religion.

What purpose then does the Church serve? We sometimes want it to be more, and sometimes less, than it is. The Church was not designed like a Swiss Army Knife, with a tool to meet every need, a program to serve every function.[6] We often impose on the Church organization similar expectations, wanting it to fulfill purposes it was never intended to serve. At the same time, we often bridle against the programs, manuals, cultural accretions, and institutional practices that can seem like distractions at best and spiritual impediments at worst. In the first century, the first great controversies in the church in Palestine were rooted in this very dilemma: what parts of the Jewish context and heritage in which Christianity took root properly pertain to the eternal gospel, and which features are expendable, culturally variable, or prophetically fulfilled and no longer essential? In the book of Acts we read of a "great dissension" that broke out on this question, as that small Galilean sect first began its long progress to becoming a global religion. "You are not Christians 'after the manner of Moses,'" some of the old crowd protested, regarding foreign converts. Peter's admonition to his fellow apostles and elders still rings with relevance today: "Now therefore why . . . put a yoke upon the neck of the disciples, which neither our fathers nor we were able to bear?"[7]

In moments of frustration it is easy to imagine a religious life unencumbered by fallible human agents, institutional forms, rules and prohibitions, cultural group-think and expected conformity to norms. As if our natural, default, primal mode were blissful freedom and natural, spontaneous joy—and it is the artificial strictures of institutional religion that get in the way! But religious forms are necessary—just not in the ways we might have conceived.

On the occasion of the Last Supper, and knowing He would not remain in person to shepherd His disciples to eternal life, Jesus instituted a practice to keep them centered and mindful of their faith's core. "This do in remembrance of me," He said in consecrating the symbols of His own broken and bleeding body, sacrificed on our behalf.[8] Then, praying for His disciples, He indicated precisely what His hope was for them in His absence. He prayed for their unity ("that they may be one, even as we are"), their sanctification ("sanctify them through thy truth"), and their perfection ("that they may be made perfect"). Presumably, the symbolism He instituted in the Last Supper was related to what He prayed would be their destiny, the effects it pointed them toward. Partaking of the sacrament, mindful of its meaning, was intended to move them toward greater unity with their fellow believers—in similitude of Christ's unity with the Father—growing holiness, and eventual return to the Divine Family. Problems enter into our understanding of the Church when we divorce the first part of Christ's model of true religion, the Lord's Supper, from the second part, the effects it should generate. Clearly He wanted to suggest that remembering His selflessness and service, His *enacted* and not merely *verbal* expression of love, was the key to perfect oneness of heart. The power to unite, to sanctify, and to perfect, in other words, is rooted in Christ's sacrifice and its emulation by His disciples.

41

To put this more simply, the purposes for which we go to church should be to reenact, in microcosm, the motivations and objectives that Jesus had in laying down His life for us. By coming together in community, serving and ministering to each other, sacrificing self-lessly and loving unfailingly, we grow united, sanctified, and per-fected in the family of Christ. As the moral lesson without paral-lel and the basis of our own salvation and the world's hope, the Atonement fittingly serves as the focal point of our Sunday worship.

Most of us get this, if only vaguely. We know that the main pur-pose of Sabbath observance is to partake of the Lord's Supper. But we sometimes grow frustrated with all the peripherals. Lessons and talks are to some Mormons what cafeteria food is to teenagers—not just in the way they can be bland and boring, but in the way that they sometimes bring us together in mutual griping rather than mu-tual edification. But what if we saw lessons and talks as connections to the sacrament rather than as unrelated secondary activities? What if we saw them as opportunities to bear with one another in all our infirmities and ineptitude? What if we saw the mediocre talk, the overbearing counselor, the lesson read straight from the manual, as a lay member's equivalent of the widow's mite? A humble offer-ing, perhaps, but one to be measured in terms of the capacity of the giver rather than in the value received. And if the effort itself is negligible—well, then the gift is the opportunity given us to exercise patience and mercy. If that sounds too idealistic, if we insist on im-posing a higher standard on our co-worshippers, if we insist on mea-suring our worship service in terms of what we "get out of" the meet-ing, then perhaps we have erred in our understanding of worship.

The first time the word *worship* appears in the King James Version of the Old Testament, it appears with appalling import. "Abide ye here," Abraham tells his servant, while "I and the lad will go yonder and worship."[9] The terrible offering of his son's life is what the Bible's first instance of "worship" portends. In the New Testament, the word *worship* first appears again in conjunction with a costly offering. It is used in reference to the wise men, who "worshipped" the Christ child by "open[ing] their treasures" and "present[ing] unto him gifts."[10] Worship, then, is about what we are prepared to relinquish—what we give up at personal cost. When, in the Old Testament, King David sins against God, the prophet Gad tells him to offer a sacrifice by way of reconciliation. Hearing of this, a well-intentioned King Araunah offers to ease David's burden by providing both the site for the altar and the sacrificial oxen. David reproves him, asking, how can "I offer burnt offerings unto the Lord my God of that which doth cost me nothing"?[11] Abraham, the wise men, and King David understood that in true worship, we approach the Divine with the desire to offer treasures and gifts, not to seek them.

COMMUNITY

But can we not find a framework for giving of self, for service, in any number of settings? Of course we can. The Church offers a particular kind of community that is irreplaceable and particular vehicles of grace that are indispensable. First, the Church is a community. In the logic of Zion building, Saints build heaven where they find themselves gathered; they do not go in search of the heavenly city—or a more heavenly congregation. Thus, Zion building continues to have precisely determined geographical referents. The shopping around for more satisfying spiritual nourishment has long been a heritage of the Protestant Reformation—so much so that in 1559, the Act of Uniformity required all English people to attend their own parish churches. Today that requirement is little more than a quaint memory of a time before religious association and attendance became products of market forces. Mormon practice has achieved what the English parliament could not. With the rarest of exceptions, Mormons attend the ward where they find themselves geographically situated. They are perhaps the last Christian church to do so with consistency.

It would be hard to overestimate the impact this physical boundedness has on the shaping of Mormon culture. Like the family into which one is born, wards become the inescapable condition of a Mormon's social and spiritual life. Just as, ironically, siblings forge fiercer bonds of loyalty and love to those with whom they never freely chose to associate, so does the arbitrariness of ward boundaries create a virtual inevitability about the ward's cohesion. Congregations and their bishops do not audition for new adherents' willful association. They are instantaneously designated a new move-in's adoptive family, without the member's right of dissent or appeal.

Although not all family relations are idyllic, most are remarkably strong and a primary source for the individual's identity. Surely that is, in part, a function of the cost individuals pay to make a relationship work. Love is a product of what we put into a relationship. We love our families because of how much we have invested in them, how many times we fought, argued, simmered, and stewed but were forced back to the negotiating table by an unavoidable proximity and by a connection that transcended personal choice. We love that irritating brother and that infuriating sister because we couldn't simply walk away in a moment of frustration. We had to submit to the hard schooling of love because we couldn't transfer to another class with siblings more to our taste. As the German theologian Dietrich Bonhöffer realized, "cheap grace is the mortal enemy of the church," and one version of cheap grace is "baptism without the discipline of community."[12]

Like Robinson Crusoe on his island, Mormons implicitly recognize that any resources they need to employ for the building of Zion must be found within themselves or their immediate environs, not among more congenial fellow Saints or under the tutelage of more inspiring leaders the next block over. These wards and stakes thus function as laboratories and practicums where we discover that we love God by learning to love each other.

ORDINANCES

Second, the Church is a vehicle of grace. Most humans experience the insufficiency of their own efforts to find peace and holiness. Some find a satisfactory self-sufficiency, and some die in that condition of contentment. But most of us experience, in foxholes, waiting rooms, or lonely nights, our own dark night of the soul. It may be a recognition of our repeated failure to overcome the simplest nagging foibles that cleave to our nature like barnacles on our soul's hull; we may find it in a spirit broken by our impotence in the face of the suffering of those we love. But most of us know what it is to be a branch cut off from the True Vine, to have experienced the prayer of George Herbert that "if goodness leade [me] not, yet wearinesse may tosse [me] to [thy] breast."[13] And if our faith in Jesus Christ has not dimmed completely, we will sense the healing balm offered by His Atonement, by our memory that—whatever its ultimate theological or metaphysical significance—Christ's death on the cross was the life-giving enactment of our Lord's perfect love, His choice to suffer with and for us. And the moment most conducive to the memory of that gift—the most perfect portal to its meaning and effect—is when we see His body symbolically broken anew, see His blood ritually offered again, and bow in remembrance. That is the moment, in the presence of that offering, that we make our own sacrifice. There, in true worship, we complete the ritual by offering our most costly gifts—our debilitating predilections and habits. "I will give away all my sins to know thee,"[14] said the Lamanite king. We know these are our most precious possessions, or we would not hold onto them so tenaciously and for so long. The sacrament is the setting and occasion to complete that transaction, the supreme moment of worship—and it cannot be replicated in any personal religion we fashion on our own.

And there is yet a second set of ordinances that constitute the ultimate purpose of the Church. In 1636, in the beautiful cathedral in York, the grieving widower Phineas Hodson erected a small brass plaque, expressing his hope "to be re-united with her in bliss who now hears not when he calls."[15] Millions of men and women have lived and died in the fervent hope of reunion with departed family and beloved friends. The temple, for those who believe, is the sacred place where fond hopes find tangible enactment. But why should such formality be required? Why can God not simply reunite all the faithful, or open the doors of heaven to the entire human family?

One possible explanation is that, simply put, those questions misconstrue the nature of heaven. To ask them is, once again, to ask the wrong question. It is to make any number of assumptions about heaven that a little thought will not bear out. Heaven is not a location to which good people are assigned, and salvation is not a simple condition of perfect righteousness. The goal of human striving, according to the New Testament, is the acquisition of eternal life—which may be read to mean, the attainment of the kind of life that God Himself leads and enjoys. And that is not simply an existence defined by His perfect attributes. God is God by virtue of the perfection of the *relationships* He has founded and preserved. He has "set his heart" upon us, "doeth not anything save it be for [our] benefit," weeps over our suffering in sin, and makes it His personal work and glory to bring about our exaltation.[16] Clearly, heaven is a complete immersion—a full engagement and participation in a web of eternal, familial bonds of love and affection.

Here, however, is the surprising implication of that insight. The most perfect man or woman—the one who embodies the most perfect honesty, humility, purity, wisdom, kindness—is not necessarily or therefore in relationship with anyone or any God. As Ryan Davis has argued, perfect compliance with moral law, in other words, does not of itself create the sociability of which heaven consists. Being a good person doesn't of itself put us into meaningful relationship with anyone. That is why, according to Joseph Smith's magnificent vision of the heavenly kingdoms, the honorable men and women of the earth are saved in a kingdom of glory but are not in the Father's presence: not because they do not "deserve" it or qualify for it but because, given the opportunity, they did not create that relationship.[17]

Relationships are constructed out of interactions, reciprocal expressions of love, shared purpose, and mutual commitments. We forge relationships with individuals interpersonally in the world of action, not privately in the chambers of our own conscience or by habits of moral reflection. Acquired attributes of godliness are not themselves constitutive of any relationship. Personal holiness is a *precondition* for living in the presence of a Being who is compared to "devouring fire" and "everlasting burnings."[18] But holiness does not itself constitute a relationship with that Being. Personal gestures of love and devotion, obedience born of fondness and friendship, do. In earthly domains, as in heavenly kingdoms, we create meaningful bonds and connections by what we specifically do with, for, and at the behest of the other.

The complaint that ordinances of salvation are arbitrary misses the point. They are arbitrary in order to fulfill their purpose. In C. S. Lewis's masterful retelling of the "Fall," an angel in human form explains to Eve's counterpart why some commandments seem random, capricious. "Where can you taste the joy of obeying," he asks, "unless He bids you do something for which His bidding is the only reason?"[19] In this light and context, the seeming arbitrariness of gospel ordinances becomes the very ground on which the particularism of a specific, personal relationship with the Divine becomes enacted. Ordinances make possible our response to God's invitation. We are enabled to formalize and constitute a living, dynamic relationship through a set of ritual performances. We willfully and bodily participate in the forging of that relationship as a response to a personal beckoning rather than an impersonal moral imperative. Through baptism, we formally and publicly accept Christ's invitation to be our spiritual Father. We thus signal our desire to be adopted into His family. Through the endowment, we affirm our commitment to bind ourselves more closely to Him through progressively greater demonstrations of our love and fidelity. And in our own temple sealing, we signify our willingness to expand the intimate association with the Divine, both laterally through marriage and vertically through posterity.

From another angle, what at times could appear empty legalism might in a broader context be seen as an alternative to the well-intentioned but disastrous illusion of an ungrounded human autonomy. The ordinances—like the structures of organized religion themselves—provide an unchanging framework giving continuity to our relationship to the Divine. God not only revealed all the ordinances of salvation to Adam, Joseph taught, but intended them "to be the same forever, and set Adam to watch over them [and] to reveal them from heaven to man or to send Angels to reveal them" in the event of their loss.[20] Their unvarying employment was the token of a covenant that binds us to premortal conventions we participated in creating; they constitute "the most perfect order and harmony—and their limits and bounds were fixed irrevocably and voluntarily subscribed to."[21] This is why, in Joseph's words, we "have got to be subject to certain rules & principles" established "before the world was."[22]

Wordsworth found that the rules of sonnet making do not in fact constrain, but actually make possible, poetic form. Beauty, he found, comes with the exercise of freedom within particular bounds. So might we find in ordinances an empowerment in our quest to be disciples. In so doing we might feel to say, as Wordsworth concludes, "some Souls . . . who have felt the weight of too much liberty, should find brief solace there, as I have found."

In ancient Israel, the Sadducees were the guardians of the temple, "cherishing the highest regard" for the Lord's house and the things of eternal meaning that transpired therein.[23] Religion without those institutional forms that give us the means to formalize, to concretize, and to strengthen our bonds with each other and with loving Heavenly Parents would be only an alluring promise devoid of substance.

CHAPTER 4

OF CANONS AND CANNONS:

THE USE AND ABUSE OF SCRIPTURE

———•———

The Bible is an antique volume
Written by faded men,
At the suggestion of Holy Spectres—
Subjects—Bethlehem—
Eden—the ancient Homestead—
Satan—the Brigadier,
Judas—the great Defaulter,
David—the Troubadour.
Sin—a distinguished Precipice
Others must resist,
Boys that "believe"
Are very lonesome—
Other boys are "lost."
Had but the tale a warbling Teller
All the boys would come—
Orpheus' sermon captivated,
It did not condemn.

—EMILY DICKINSON[1]

canon, *noun*

Pronunciation: /ˈkænən/

4. The collection or list of books of the Bible accepted by the Christian Church as genuine and inspired. Also, any set of sacred books.

cannon, *noun*

Pronunciation: /ˈkænən/

2 a. A piece of ordnance; a gun or firearm of a size which requires it to be mounted for firing.[2]

T he root of the word *canon* suggests a standard of measurement. A canon represents a rule or guide that is authoritative, especially in matters of spiritual life. Church laws and statutes are part of "canon law," and by "the canon" we understand a set of holy books. The original meaning of authoritative rule or teaching persists in the equivalent expression, the *standard* works. In discipleship, the canon is what we measure ourselves by. The scriptures, said Paul to Timothy, are given for "correction" and "instruction in righteousness."[3] They are likened by the Psalmist to a lamp that illuminates, that lights our path.[4] Scriptures beckon, inspire, and edify.

A cannon is a different thing altogether.

The etymology of *cannon* refers to a large barrel or tube through which objects are propelled to deadly effect. It can be used offensively or defensively, but it is a weapon, meant to bludgeon into submission. Some people use the scriptural canon with the first meaning in mind. And some with the second.

Henry VIII saw "cannon" when he read "canon"; he used the scriptures rather more as a weapon than as a spiritual guide. Henry's brother, Prince Arthur, died months after his marriage to Catherine of Aragon. For reasons of political expediency, it was thought a good idea for Henry, next in line to the throne, to marry Arthur's widow—but it was against church law for a man to marry his brother's widow. So the Tudors petitioned the Pope for a dispensation, or an exemption from the rule. They had a useful scripture to suit their purposes: The Deuteronomic law had stipulated that "If brethren dwell together, and one of them die, . . . her husband's brother shall . . . take her to him to wife."[5] The dispensation was granted, and Henry married Catherine.

Some years later, Henry had tired of his wife, who had failed in any case to produce the desired heir he needed to ensure a smooth succession and stabilize the kingdom. So, Henry petitioned the Pope for an annulment. Once again, he found a perfect scripture to suit his purpose. Leviticus 18 had commanded that "thou shalt not uncover the nakedness of thy brother's wife,"[6] which most commentators took to mean, you shall not wed your brother's widow.

For the next several years, bishops, lawyers, theologians, and king's counselors furiously contended over the contradictory biblical verses. The kingdom was roiled, the church was riven, and heads rolled. What is clear amidst the havoc that followed is that the king was not—in the case of his marriage to Catherine or in the case of his petition for divorce—using the Bible as a spiritual guide. He was using it as a weapon to justify his dynastic—and amorous—interests. *Cannon*, not *canon*, was the operative term, and armed with his scriptural arsenal he blasted his way to ecclesiastical supremacy and a new marriage to Anne Boleyn.

This would not be the first or the last time that competing scriptural injunctions led to fractures in Christendom. The logic of the Reformation spearheaded by Martin Luther had depended in large measure on perceived discrepancies between Paul and James. Seeing that the Bible was not always in harmony with itself, Luther admonished his readers to "discriminate between all the books and decide which are the best."[7] He ranked Paul higher than James, which is why he made the words of the former, "The just shall live by faith," the theological foundation for the Reformation he launched.[8] Considering the letter of James to be an epistle full "of straw" by comparison made it easier to downplay that apostle's claim that "faith without works is dead."[9]

As individuals, we also are apt to use the canon as a cannon. We invoke the stripling warriors of Helaman and the iron rod of Lehi's vision to ground our own version of unflinching obedience. Or we invoke the lessons of the Liahona to support our more spontaneous and flexible approach to gospel living. In America, some Mormons find Jesus' ministry to the downtrodden and King Benjamin's words about withholding judgment but not relief from the beggar to be apt endorsement of their preferred political policies. At the other end of the spectrum, some invoke the war in heaven fought over agency and consider the Mormon ethic of self-reliance to be adequate support for a different political outlook. Or, sometimes individuals even employ the cannon *against* the canon, citing inconsistencies and imperfections in the record as grounds for nonbelief in the principle of inspiration, one's faith tradition, or even God.

This is lamentable, but fully understandable. Some are dismayed that a supposedly loving God is sometimes portrayed in scripture as wrathful, vindictive, and unfair. They might quote verses to their purposes, invoking the Lord's own words regarding persecutors of the Saints: "Cursed are all those that shall lift up the heel against mine anointed. . . . They shall not have right to the priesthood, nor their posterity after them from generation to generation."[10] What kind of a God, one might protest, punishes children for unrighteous ancestors? Searching for a God who is merciful and just, others would point to verse 20 of the "cursing," which notes that "they themselves shall be despised by those that flattered them," indicating that God is describing the natural consequences of a life of perfidy, not acting as an agent of retribution.

Similarly, some may point to Christ turning over the tables of the money changers to support a view that even Jesus showed moments of wrath. But then, one might note in the same story that only "when he had made a scourge of small cords" did He disrupt the commerce taking place. John adds the detail, one can reasonably infer, to indicate Christ's perfect control and considered response rather than impulsive rage.[11]

These examples suggest that many scriptural contradictions are only apparent, evaporating upon closer or more contextualized reading. But other examples, like those employed by King Henry, are more resistant to reconciliation. God is not a man that He should "change his mind," we read in Numbers 23:19 (NRSV). But a few books later, Jeremiah insists that if the people repent, "the Lord will change his mind" (Jeremiah 26:13, NRSV). Judas hangs himself in Matthew, but he falls headlong and dies in Acts. Jehoiachin was eighteen years old when he began to reign according to one chronicler, but eight years old according to another. "Answer a fool according to his folly," we are admonished in one Proverb; but another verse had already instructed us, "Answer *not* a fool according to his folly."[12]

The question is, what do we do with these internal scriptural contradictions? Joseph Smith was speaking in relative terms when he said the Book of Mormon was the "most correct book." Even in that scriptural record, Nephi reminded readers that if he erred as author, so "did they err of old."[13] And the other scriptures would presumably be "less correct" if the Book of Mormon were "the most correct." If the Bible is only the word of God "as far as it is translated correctly," then clearly it is not the word of God in every aspect of its present form. If many "plain and precious things" were removed,[14] then many plain and precious things are missing. And as nature abhors a vacuum, it is likely those gaps were filled with things that are neither plain nor precious. Joseph Smith said the Song of Solomon did not constitute "inspired writings," and urged his listeners to use discretion, wisdom, and inspiration in how they read the scriptures. On the other hand, one of Joseph's revelations encouraged Latter-day Saints to study the Apocrypha, because "there are many things contained therein that are true."[15]

"Some will say, the scriptures say so & so," he told a large congregation with some impatience. But "I have the oldest Book in the world [the Bible] & the Holy Ghost I thank God for the old Book but more for the Holy Ghost. . . . If ye are not led by revelation how can ye escape the damnation of Hell."[16]

One lesson Latter-day Saints should take from all this is the greater responsibility to model Joseph's practice of combining spiritual guidance with intellectual effort to discern the Divine voice. In searching the scriptures, we should expect to find pearls amidst the detritus of the centuries. It is certainly the case, as many troubled readers have noticed, that in the five books of Moses and elsewhere, some portions of scripture portray a kinder, gentler God, while others depict a God who orders wholesale slaughter of non-Israelites. Contradictions in the text are not contradictions in the nature of God Himself, and readers must spiritually discern for themselves the reason for the inconsistencies. As Joseph Smith said, "many things in the scriptures . . . do not, as they now stand, accord with the revelation of the Holy Ghost to me."[17] Specifically, that revelation included a clearer picture of the true nature of God, which early Church leaders called absolutely "necessary in order that any rational and intelligent being may exercise faith in God unto life and salvation."[18] It is striking that scholars too find very different conceptions of Deity coming from different sections and passages of the Old Testament. Some are much closer than others to the weeping God revealed to Enoch.

For instance, the biblical scholar Richard Elliott Friedman notes that "probably the most remarkable difference of all" in disparate passages "is their different ways of picturing God." Some depict "a deity who can regret things that he has done ([Gen.] 6:6, 7), . . . a deity who can be 'grieved to his heart' (6:6). . . . This anthropomorphic quality . . . is virtually entirely lacking in other passages."[19] The great Jewish scholar Abraham Heschel similarly finds moments when a God of empathy and vulnerability shines through the text. This is the God who says of sorrowing Israel, not simply "I *know* their sufferings," as the inadequate translation renders it, but "I *have sympathy for*, I *am affected by*, their sufferings."[20] Rather than surrendering to the varying moments of tension and disagreement in the scriptural record, it might be well to remember Jesus's reproof of His contemporaries. We need to *search* the scriptures in the company of the Holy Ghost. Reading them merely is insufficient to reveal the portions that most truly testify of Christ and His Father.

In sum, disciples might do well to avoid the bibliolatry that characterizes scripture as unerring truth. Parley Pratt made this point himself in *The Fountain of Knowledge*, a small pamphlet he wrote in 1844. With elegant metaphor, he noted that scripture resulted from revelatory process and was thus the product of revealed truth, not the other way around. We do well to look to a stream for nourishing water, but we do better to secure the fountain. That fountain, Pratt noted, is "the gift of revelation," which "the restoration of all things" heralds.[21] Or, in George MacDonald's metaphor, we should hold the scriptures as "the moon of our darkness, . . . not dear as the sun towards which we haste."[22]

Biblical inconsistencies, common sense, the Book of Mormon's own words, and Joseph Smith's remarks on the subject make it difficult for Mormons to be strict scriptural literalists. The reason for scriptural imperfection should be obvious: scripture comes to us through human conduits. The Doctrine and Covenants defines scripture as that which is spoken by godly people "as they are moved upon by the Holy Ghost."[23] This does not suggest a process by which a prophet invariably takes dictation as the Lord verbally recites a set of verses. The variety of prophetic utterance, the assortment of genres and categories, the array of circumstances and conditions under which scripture came to be recorded and canonized admit of no such simplistic view. God may have written with His finger on Mt. Sinai, but it is Paul who writes a formal epistle to saints in Corinth. Court chroniclers record the details of the reigns of Jewish rulers. Psalmists record poetic words of celebration and praise. Nephi relates his family history. Joseph Smith writes a personal letter filled with pain and yearning from a Missouri jail cell. All partake in varying degrees of heavenly inspiration; all bear the human traces of those who felt the Spirit move upon them; all are filtered through an individual's mind and cultural environment.

"The things of God are of deep import, and time, and experience, and careful, and solemn, and ponderous thoughts can only find them out," Joseph said.[24] He was willing to put in the time, and the painstaking effort, to understand the things of God. He studied German so he could read Luther's superb translation of the scriptures. He studied Hebrew so he could get closer to the original text of the Old Testament. Notwithstanding his calling as a seer, he labored to understand Egyptian as he worked his way through the papyri that led to his production of the Book of Abraham.

All of which is to say, we need to search the scriptures *and* rely upon the Spirit to discern the true God and His true nature. When dissonance and distress set in, we should trust in the Spirit to find the hidden God of scripture, the One who knows us by name, who weeps with us in our pain, and who has graven us on the palms of His hands.

CHAPTER 5

ON PROPHECY AND PROPHETS:
THE PERILS OF HERO WORSHIP

—————•—————

Yet have I often seen, by cunning hand,
And force of fire, what curious things are made
Of wretched earth. . . .
But since those great ones, be they ne'er so great,
Come from the earth, . . .
I do not greatly wonder at the sight,
If earth in earth delight.

—GEORGE HERBERT[1]

"I am the least in my [family]," said Gideon (Judges 6:15).

"I . . . am but a lad, . . . and all the people hate me," said Enoch (Moses 6:31).

"I am a man of unclean lips," said Isaiah (Isaiah 6:5).

"I am slow of speech, and of a slow tongue," said Moses (Exodus 4:10).

"Jonah set out to flee . . . from the presence of the Lord" (Jonah 1:3).

Dostoevsky believed that "man, so long as he remains free, has no more constant and agonizing anxiety than to find as quickly as possible someone to worship."[2] His contemporary, the great nineteenth-century man of letters Thomas Carlyle, was convinced that hero worship would last for as long as the human race endured. "Heroes, it would seem, exist always, and a certain worship of them. . . . Hero worship cannot cease till man himself ceases. . . . Hero worship [is] indestructible."[3] Carlyle didn't think that was a bad thing. For he believed that "great men" of history were the mobilizers of the human race: "They were the leaders of men, these great ones; the modellers, patterns, and in a wide sense creators, of whatsoever the general mass of men contrived to do or to attain."[4]

This may be true. History has largely been shaped by visionaries and madmen, by saints and megalomaniacs, by men and women with the charisma, the energy, and the titanic confidence to build pyramids, forge empires, and found world faiths. Carlyle saw the power and potential that reside in the heroic. Great leaders do not just shape the course of history, they awaken and unleash tremendous forces that generally lie dormant in the individual human soul. For if the spark of divinity animates every man and woman, it is too often obscured by the monotonous daily grind of economic and emotional survival, buried beneath fear and doubts and life's teeming distractions or simple inertia. *Dry kindling* is what Carlyle called such untapped human resource, waiting for holy fire from heaven to ignite it, waiting for those who can deliver "spiritual lightning."[5] In this view, heroic figures perform their most important work when they serve as a great lodestone, aligning human potential toward its true north, drawing forth the best and noblest desires and predispositions of the soul. Noble heroes, with a thousand or a million disciples energized and responsive to their clarion call, have already transformed the human souls of many even before they turn the people's energies to rebuilding Eden. True leaders orient disciples toward the Divine. That is the beauty and the power of their leadership.

The great writer Dostoevsky agreed with Carlyle about the human propensity to admire heroes—even to worship them. As he recognized, "for the humble soul . . . , worn out by toil and grief and, above all, by everlasting injustice and everlasting sin, both his own and the world's, there was no greater need and comfort than to find some holy shrine or person, to fall down before him and worship him."[6] However, within that description of ready discipleship is the key to its lurking danger. We may think the call to follow is an incitement to a great cause or project, one that requires devotion and sacrifice and submission. And the call of Jesus to "come and follow me"[7] is just that. But, too often, we confuse the call to discipleship with the desire to unload responsibility for our spiritual direction onto another. Christ invites us to assume the yoke, but we would rather ride in the cart. *That* is one reason why some find comfort in hero worship. It represents a release from the burden of responsibility. In Dostoevsky's words, whereas many of the devout are convinced they are seeking the Good, the True, the Holy, they are in actual fact seeking something else: "someone to keep [their] conscience."[8]

True prophets have always resisted that role. They have steadfastly refused to be the keepers of an individual's conscience. Brigham Young protested the perils of slavish obedience and submission: "I do not wish any Latter-day Saint in this world, nor in heaven, to be satisfied with anything I do, unless the Spirit of the Lord Jesus Christ, the spirit of revelation, makes them satisfied. *I wish them to know for themselves and understand for themselves.*"[9] Elsewhere he reaffirmed: "I am more afraid that this people have so much confidence in their leaders that they will not inquire for themselves of God whether they are led by him. I am fearful that they settle down in a state of blind self-security, trusting their eternal destiny in the hands of their leaders with a reckless confidence that in itself would thwa[r]t the purposes of God. . . . Let every man and woman know, by the whispering of the Spirit of God to themselves, whether their leaders are walking in the path the Lord dictates, or not."[10]

His beloved younger colleague, the colorful J. Golden Kimball, reminded his audience that "There are not enough Apostles in the Church to prevent us from thinking, and they are not disposed to do so; but some people fancy that because we have the Presidency and Apostles of the Church that they will do the thinking for us. There are men and women so mentally lazy that they hardly think for themselves. To think calls for effort, which makes some men tired and wearies their souls. No man or woman can remain in this Church on borrowed light."[11] However, in 1945, a Church magazine urged upon its readers the exact opposite, that "When our leaders speak, the thinking has been done." Many are familiar with that expression; fewer are aware that when President George Albert Smith learned of it, he immediately and indignantly repudiated the statement. "Even to imply that members of the Church are not to do their own thinking," he wrote, "is grossly to misrepresent the true ideal of the Church."[12]

Regrettably, this myth persists in the minds of many Latter-day Saints, even as leaders disavow infallibility and urge upon members personal responsibility. "Not every statement made by a Church leader, past or present, necessarily constitutes doctrine," reminded Elder Todd Christofferson.[13] When a member of the First Presidency recently expressed what should have been an unexceptional truism—"leaders in the Church have simply made mistakes"—the *New York Times* found it unusual enough to devote two articles to it.[14] Even the best, and best-intentioned, men and women called by God are, in the end, human vessels.

The scriptures themselves, even as they paint inspiring pictures of the faithfulness of God's chosen leaders, are surprisingly frank about their foibles. Abraham was less than fully honest about Sarai being his sister. Sarai treated her handmaid with jealousy that escalated to brutality. Jacob, aided and abetted by Rebekah, deceived his father, Isaac, and brother, Esau, to obtain both the latter's birthright and his blessing. Moses was guilty of manslaughter in killing an Egyptian; then he covered up his crime.[15] He also took glory unto himself at the waters of Meribah and was punished severely as a consequence.[16] Jonah ignored the Lord's call, then embarrassed himself in a pageant of self-pity because God didn't burn Nineveh to the ground as He had threatened.[17] It doesn't get a lot better in the New Testament. Apostles squabbled over which of them would receive highest honors in heaven, and the pugnacious Paul rebuked Peter sharply for what he called "fear" and "hypocrisy" in his refusal to embrace the gentiles as equals.[18] Then Paul argued with fellow apostle Barnabas, and the "contention was so sharp" that they parted company.[19]

Nor did Joseph Smith claim to be holier than the people he led. On one occasion, he said emphatically, "I don't want you to think I am very righteous, for I am not very righteous."[20] Another time, he

64

admitted, "I frequently fell into many foolish errors, and displayed the weakness of youth, and the corruption of human nature."[21] To drive home the point, he canonized those scriptures in which he was rebuked for his inconstancy and weakness: "How oft you have transgressed the commandments and the laws of God," the Lord told him.[22] He "feared man more than God," and went "on in the persuasions of men," and was chastised as "not excusable in [his] transgressions."[23] Those who knew Joseph best loved and respected him, but they harbored no delusions about his flaws. "I saw the . . . imperfections in him," said Lorenzo Snow. Brigham Young was of the same mind: "I admitted in my feelings and knew all the time that Joseph was a human being and subject to err. . . . He had his weakness," he noted. "Still it was none of my business to look after his faults."[24]

Some believe God could, and should, do better. Surely God could find more saintly vessels to carry out His work, they suppose. Many of our expectations about human institutions are so predicated on meritocracy that we are sure God must operate the same way. The head of the corporation should be the most talented business leader. The orchestra's concertmaster should be the most skillful violinist. The starting quarterback is the one who plays the best football. Surely the leaders of the Church should be the most righteous and flawless of humans!

It is helpful to remember that it is more important for disciples to be motivated than to be awestruck. As Lorenzo Snow wisely noted, "I thanked God that He would put upon a man who had those imperfections the power and authority He placed upon him for I knew that I myself had weakness[es], and I thought there was a chance for me." That is why "I thanked God that I saw these imperfections."[25] There is a reason why every man and woman may hold leadership positions: a lay church drives home the point that all are equally members of the body of Christ, that all should have equal access to spiritual gifts and heavenly powers. In 1838, anti-Mormon crusader La Roy Sunderland published a multipart attack on the faith in his publication *Zion's Watchman*. He was indignant over the Latter-day Saint Church's teaching that we could literally, in Peter's words, acquire "the divine nature."[26] Parley Pratt responded to the criticisms with his own pamphlet. He believed that rather than fawning choirs of angels, God wanted us all to be joint-heirs with Christ, a doctrine he considered Mormonism's most magnificent. He celebrated what he called "this doctrine of equality."[27]

A second reason for God's choice of fallible leaders is simply this: He has no other kind. The most holy of men and women have their feet of clay. Erecting any—even the noblest among us—into an idol is both dangerous and a fail-safe recipe for disappointment. From God's perspective, the problem is not the universality of human weakness; it is the universality of human trust in that weakness. He doesn't warn against trusting in flawed flesh, but in human flesh. "Cursed is he that putteth his trust in the arm of flesh," writes Nephi. Any *human* flesh; that is the point. "I will trust in *thee*," pledges the insightful Nephi.[28] When Neal Maxwell compared mortality to a laboratory in which we practice on each other, he likened the membership to "clinical material" at risk from inexpert practitioners.[29] But the harder thing to remember is that we are *all* interns, this side of Zion, laity and leaders alike. As Edward Beecher wrote, *all* humans participate in this "moral hospital" called the world.[30] And we will all bear the wounds we inflict, wittingly or unwittingly, upon each other.

Which leads to the third reason God employs flawed vessels: to help redirect our attention in the right direction. The story of Gideon illustrates this principle. The Lord summons the young warrior Gideon to free Israel from oppression at the hands of the Midianites. Not coincidentally, the sin that has brought about Israel's predicament was the sin of idolatry. Gideon raises an army of thirty-two thousand men and prepares for battle, but the Lord interrupts his plans. Your army is too big, He advises. Proceeding with such a host, if they triumph, they will credit themselves for the victory. So Gideon pares the army down to ten thousand. Still too many, insists the Lord. Pausing the army at a watering place, Gideon further reduces their number to a paltry three hundred. With so few, their victory over the hordes of Midianites could only be attributed to Divine assistance. And that is how we usually end the story. The real end of the story, however, is tragedy, not triumph. Gideon leads his little band to battle, and they do indeed smite and scatter the camp of the Midianites. Gideon's hope is that the miraculous victory will deflect Israel's worship from the false god Baal to the true God of their fathers. Regrettably, it is not God that his army credits for the slaughter. It is Gideon: "Then the men of Israel said unto Gideon, Rule thou over us, both thou, and thy son, and thy son's son also: for *thou* hast delivered us from the hand of Midian." Gideon replies, "I will not rule over you, neither shall my son rule over you: the Lord shall rule over you."[31]

However, the predilection to revere a human leader is too great. His valorous men cannot lift their eyes further than the immediately visible—the great leader who has taken them to so stupendous a victory. As for Gideon, he falls prey to the resulting adulation and riches. He fashions a cult object with his newfound wealth, which inevitably becomes "a snare unto Gideon, and to his house."[32] Perhaps it was for this reason—to encourage disciples to look to the Lord for redemption—that Joseph Smith was careful to have the following recorded in the Doctrine and Covenants: "For unto this end have I raised you [Joseph] up, that I might show forth my wisdom through the *weak* things of the earth."[33]

The notion that modern-day prophets are infallible specimens of virtue and perfection is neither scriptural nor reasonable. They are simply ordinary women and men who have accepted the call and are striving to return Home, as we all are. Equally unreasonable is a view of published revelation as infallible, unerring transmission of the Divine voice. A simplistic notion of modern prophets as stenographers of Deity is not what the prophetic tradition, ancient or modern, suggests. President Wilford Woodruff spoke about revelation—and Restoration—as ongoing processes rather than events. Noting how Mormon understanding of temple work and temple sealings evolved over time, he had this to say in 1894: "We have felt there was more to be revealed upon this subject than we had received." Changes came as revelation unfolded, he said, and "we still have more changes to make in order to satisfy our Heavenly Father. . . . We have felt, as President Taylor said, that we have got to have more revelation concerning sealing."[34] Translating God's will into specific programs, policies, and practices, in other words, requires ongoing effort. One of the greatest Jewish scholars writes, "An analysis of prophetic utterances shows that the fundamental experience of the prophet is a fellowship with the feelings of God. . . . The prophet hears God's voice and feels His heart. He tries to impart the pathos of the message."[35]

Joseph Smith's manuscript revelations similarly reveal a man ever struggling to find the right language to convey the truths that he sensed in his communion with the Divine. In recent years, the historical department of the Church has produced documentary editions of those revelations. Most of the manuscript versions show more editorial changes, before the revelation made its way into print, than many an author's literary manuscript. It is clear that Joseph did not wish to promote the idea of himself as an infallible oracle, transmitting with pristine perfection the word of God. For there in the Facsimile Edition of the Joseph Smith Papers, published by the Church for all the world to see in half a dozen vivid colors, are the additions, strike-outs, and rewordings to Joseph's original words made by half a dozen different hands, his own included.[36]

Whatever spiritual intimations he received of God's mind and will, however powerful the fonts of inspiration at which he drank, Joseph had to transmit eternal things into the idiom of common English. And that, he found, was no easy task. As he complained to a friend, "Oh Lord God, deliver us from this prison, . . . of a crooked, broken, scattered and imperfect language."[37] And so he related both the epiphanies of celestial brilliance and the merest glimmers of heavenly truth to ready scribes. And then he reworked the language—and enlisted other respected associates to the task of refining and remolding the wording—in an effort to depict more accurately the Divine mind and the truths the Spirit communicated as "pure intelligence flowing unto" him.[38]

Outside of Joseph's scriptural production, his words ranged from wise and inspired to simple opinion—with his audience, then as now, seldom attuned to the differences. Joseph himself complained that "he did not enjoy the right vouchsafed to every American citizen—that of free speech. He said that when he ventured to give his private opinion" about various subjects, they ended up "being given out as the word of the Lord because they came from him."[39] When not speaking with prophetic authority, in other words, he claimed no authority at all—which is why his pronouncements on subjects from Lehi's New World landfall to the prospects of the Kirtland Bank were as liable to error as other men's. Mormon leaders—like the great souls of other religious traditions—are never assured an unvarying inspiration when they speak or write.

Brigham Young frankly acknowledged the varying currents of inspiration he experienced. Elder J. Reuben Clark Jr. recounted a story told to him by his father about President Young. He said that at the time of the Utah War, Young "preached to the people in a morning meeting a sermon vibrant with defiance to the approaching army, and declaring an intention to oppose and drive them back. In the afternoon meeting he arose and said that Brigham Young had been talking in the morning, but the Lord was going to talk now. He then delivered an address, the tempo of which was the opposite from the morning talk."[40] This also explains why the apostle George Q. Cannon could say of Brigham Young, for example, that in certain instances, "Some of my brethren . . . feel that in the promulgation of doctrine he took liberties beyond those to which he was legitimately entitled."[41]

Airbrushing our leaders, past or present, is both a wrenching of the scriptural record and a form of idolatry. It generates an inaccurate paradigm that creates false expectations and disappointment. God specifically said that He called weak vessels so we wouldn't place our faith in *their* strength or power, but in God's. The prophetic mantle represents priesthood keys, not a level of holiness or infallibility. That is why our scripturally mandated duty to the prophets and apostles is not to idolize them but to uphold and sustain them "by the prayer of faith."[42] In so doing, we acknowledge Him who called them, "even with that same calling with which [Paul] was called."[43] And in so doing, we have the promise that He shall "cause the heavens to shake for [our] good, and his name's glory."[44]

CHAPTER 6

On Delegation and Discipleship:
The Ring of Pharaoh

· — · · — · ·

Wherefore I dare not, I, put forth my hand
To hold the Ark, although it seem to shake
Through th' old sinnes and new doctrines of our land.
Onely, since God doth often vessels make
Of lowly matter for high uses meet,
I throw me at his feet.

—George Herbert[1]

When Joseph of the many-colored coat had gained Pharaoh's complete trust and confidence, "Pharaoh took off his ring from his hand, and put it upon Joseph's hand."³ With this gesture, Pharaoh transferred his own power and authority to the former Hebrew slave. "Without your consent," the Pharaoh told him, "no one shall lift up hand or foot in all the land of Egypt."⁴ In the era of America's colonization, Spain and Portugal created the office of viceroy, which means literally the one "in the place or stead of the king," to describe those endowed with the king's powers, authorized to act as king in his physical absence from a new territory. To delegate is to deputize. Both words suggest more than a mere assignment or handing off of a responsibility or task. Both entail the transmission of authority that makes one an effective stand-in for the source of that authority.

Mormons frequently describe priesthood as the authority to act in God's name. But they often fail to plumb the potentially vexing implications of that principle. Authority is the source of delegation, delegation involves humans, humans entail error, and error in the context of authority creates conflict and tension. These stresses, which involve fallibility in conduct as well as in words, can be a challenge to the most faithful. Imperfect actions can be personally devastating. Knowing in theory that even those in authority over us will succumb to the same flaws and weaknesses under which we also labor does little to mitigate the pain when we suffer from poor judgment or downright unrighteousness. Teachings that seem to bear the stamp of divine authority and are later declared to be in error are even more challenging to faith.

Austin Farrer, the great Anglican churchman beloved of C. S. Lewis and often quoted by Elder Neal Maxwell, wrote an essay on "Infallibility and the Historical Tradition." Farrer's effort to balance God's divine purposes with the imperfection of His human instruments suggests one way Mormons might think about faith-wrenching practices (polygamy), missteps and errors (Adam-God), and teachings that the Church has abandoned but not fully explained (the priesthood ban). Practices, in other words, that challenge and try one's faith; teachings whose status as eternal truth is either disconcerting, questionable, or now denied. Here is what Farrer said: "Facts are not determined by authority. Authority can make law to be law; authority cannot make facts to be facts."[5] (Or, as Henry Eyring once quoted his father as saying, "in this church you don't have to believe anything that isn't true."[6])

What does it mean for us if God's anointed leader propounds what is an error? What does this mean for the truthfulness of the Church, for our duty as members and as Christian disciples? Farrer continues his meditation on the subject with a discussion of the Lord's meaning when He promised Peter that whatsoever he would bind on earth would be bound in heaven. Though he doesn't use the kind of vocabulary Mormons often employ, we might think of what Farrer says in terms of the principle of priesthood delegation of authority: "If Peter and his colleagues make law in applying the Lord's precepts, . . . their law is the law of Christ's Church, the best (if you

74

will) that God's Spirit can make with human instruments there and then, and, *as such, to be obeyed as the will of God Himself*. But to call Peter *infallible* in this connection is to misplace an epithet."[7]

This is a subtle point, but one with profoundly important implications. Delegation is a sobering, even terrifying gesture on God's part. To delegate or to deputize, both mean that the person receiving that authority has something like God's power of attorney; the person's acts, *within circumscribed limits*, carry the weight and efficacy of God's own acts. But surely no human can act with the wisdom, the perfect judgment, the infallibility of God. Precisely so. And if delegation is a real principle—if God really does endow mortals with the authority to act *in His place and with His authority*, even while He knows *they will not act with infallible judgment*—then it becomes clearer why God is asking us to receive the words of the prophet "as if from mine own mouth, *in all patience and faith*."[8] Indeed, this counsel was part of the very first revelation God gave to the newly organized Church in this dispensation, which should give the warning particular primacy among God's many counsels. Clearly, the Lord can delegate His authority to a human without any assumption that said human will always exercise that authority in perfect conformity with God's intentions. From Sunday School teachers to prophets, those with God's authority to act in His name will, even with the best of intentions and efforts, make mistakes. God has already anticipated the need to overlook His prophets' human weaknesses; hence His admonition on the day of the Church's very founding. And so did Joseph himself remind his people: "if they would bear with my infirmities . . . I would likewise bear with their infirmities," he said.[9]

However, a different question emerges when it is the action, not the person, that is imperfect. If a bishop makes a decision without inspiration, are we bound to sustain the decision? The story is told of a Church official who returned from installing a new stake presidency. "Dad, do you Brethren feel confident when you call a man as the stake president that he is the Lord's man?" the official's son asked upon his father's return home. "No, not always," he replied. "But once we call him, he becomes the Lord's man."[10] The answer disconcerts initially. Is this not hubris, to expect God's sanction for a decision made in error? Perhaps. It is also possible that the reply reveals the only understanding of delegation that is viable.

If God honored only those decisions made in perfect accord with His perfect wisdom, then His purposes would require leaders who were utterly incapable of misconstruing His intention, who never missed hearing the still small voice, who were unerringly and unfailingly a perfect conduit for heaven's inspiration. And it would render the principle of delegation inoperative. The Pharaoh didn't say to Joseph, your authority extends as far as you anticipate perfectly what I would do in every instance. He gave Joseph his ring. The king of Spain didn't say, I will honor your judgments and directives insofar as they accord with my precise conclusions at such a time as I second-guess your every word and act. He signed the viceroy's royal commission. And after calling Joseph Smith to his mission, the Lord didn't say, I will stand by you as long as you never err in judgment. He said, "Thou wast called and chosen. . . . Devote all thy service in Zion; and . . . lo, I am with thee, even unto the end."[11]

So, what does this mean for us devoted disciples of the Loving God? In Farrer's opinion, God "does not promise [Peter, or Joseph] infallible correctness in reproducing on earth the eternal decrees of heaven. *He promises him that the decisions he makes below will be sanctioned from above.*"[12] In that view, if delegation has any meaning at all, then God is as good as His word. He *honors* the words and actions of His servants, sincerely executed on His behalf. Here Farrer gives an interesting reading of Christ's words to Peter, that what His servant binds on earth, will (*then and therefore*) be bound in heaven. The words are God's promise to give His divine weight of authority to the principle of delegation, to stand surety for the leaders He entrusts.

It is at this point that the hard cases erupt into the conversation. Just how far will the Lord go in allowing a delegated authority to err? We sometimes interpret divine providence as a precisely detailed and flawlessly executed game plan. Farrer warned against the mistake of assuming "a perfect conformity of Peter's [or the prophet's] decision with a foreordaining will of God, conceived as a creative blueprint, or Platonic idea, which Peter [or the prophet] faithfully copies."[13] The Church moved to make its members' expectations in this regard more realistic when it published the sobering opinion of B. H. Roberts: "I think it is a reasonable conclusion to say that constant, never-varying inspiration is not a factor in the administration of the affairs even of the Church; not even good men, no, not though they be prophets or other high officials of the Church, are at all times and in all things inspired of God."[14] In other words, to put it starkly, God really means it when He delegates His authority to men and women—and expects them to use their wisdom and judgment in executing His will.

Does it matter that not all pronouncements will be equally inspired? It does, insofar as it creates a personal responsibility from which we cannot escape. Brigham Young feared that members would accept unthinkingly all that came from the Tabernacle pulpit. So what is the key to knowing when we may repose perfect confidence in a leader's pronouncement, and when we may not? Nathaniel Givens observed:

> As for the question of what is or is not revelation, the answer is simple. People just don't like to hear it. . . . D&C 68:4 says: "And whatsoever they shall speak when moved upon by the Holy Ghost shall be scripture, shall be the will of the Lord, shall be the mind of the Lord, shall be the word of the Lord, shall be the voice of the Lord, and the

power of God unto salvation." There's your answer and, in terms of simple language, it's not hard to understand. The problem is that it doesn't do what people want. What people want is to be absolved of responsibility. They want a formula, a rulebook, or an oracle to which they can defer tough questions. God says: "If you want to know if it's scripture or not, you're going to have to have your own connection to the Holy Ghost sufficient to figure that out." In other words: "The burden is on you." People say: "That sounds like hard work. Please give us a cheat sheet." . . . And, when God refuses to give out a cheat sheet, people just invent one. They invent doctrines of prophetic or scriptural inerrancy or sufficiency or infallibility, all of which serve more or less the exact same purpose as the original golden calf: a simulacrum of the divine that doesn't ask us to do any genuine hard work.[15]

Elder Todd Christofferson repeats counsel given earlier by J. Reuben Clark Jr. with an interesting caveat: "The Church will know by the testimony of the Holy Ghost in the body of members, whether the brethren in voicing their views are 'moved upon by the Holy Ghost': *and in due time that knowledge will be made manifest.*" Hence the "in all patience" part of the Lord's revelation on the subject.[16]

One comfort is to be found in a God whose power is in His magnanimity as well as His wisdom. These two traits mean that His divine energies are spent not in precluding chaos but in reordering it, not in preventing suffering but in alchemizing it, not in disallowing error but in transmuting it into goodness. Satan's unhindered efforts in the garden were simply assimilated into God's greater purpose. The malice of the biblical Joseph's brothers became instrumental in their entire household's salvation. ("The brothers of Joseph could have never done him so much good with their love and favor as they did him with their malice and hatred," Thomas More noted.[17]) In the supernal instance of this principle, according to the *felix culpa* of Christian tradition, the expulsion from the garden was a happy catastrophe, since it brought forth a remedy that more than compensated for the loss of Eden. Christ's sacrifice, so dazzling in its overflowing grace and mercy, made it possible for us, in leaving Eden, to return Home.

If God can transform cosmic entropy and malice alike into fire that purifies rather than destroys, how much more can He do this with the actions of well-intentioned but less-than-perfect leaders. In other words, it is reasonable to believe that in His infinite wisdom, God anticipates not only the devices and strategies of the wicked but also the foreseeable range of His leaders' errors—and appoints them with those limitations already considered. Farrer's observation is pertinent: "Doubtless, the divine will always anticipates us."[18] The Lord's words to Joseph, imprisoned in Liberty Jail, suggest such a safety net, woven of God's anticipation of and accommodation to the vicissitudes of nature and the caprice of human hearts. In spite of conspiring men and the gaping jaws of hell, Joseph is encouraged to "hold on thy way," for "their bounds are set, they cannot pass."[19] When Lehi blessed his son Jacob, he promised him that "God . . . shall consecrate thine afflictions for thy gain."[20] A brilliant truth emerges from that scripture because it lets us know that God does not send afflictions to us. Cancer, tsunamis, bad parenting, and mistakes by priesthood leaders—are all part of the mortal condition, the natural world, and the institutional Church. God's power and promise is in His capacity to transmute our suffering—and our faithful response to painful predicaments—into something beautiful. God said He would have a tried people. But He doesn't have to do the trying. We do most of it to each other—through the very weakness designed to bring us all, fallible leaders and struggling disciples, to Christ the Healer.

Eternal principles are just that—eternal and immutable.

However, hindsight shows some policies and practices to have been less immutable. In all cases, our moral responsibility as disciples varies according to our light and knowledge and a hundred other factors. It is fitting and proper, for example, that Saints through the years learned of the priesthood ban with different reactions. Those who rejected it outright may have done so believing the racial basis for exclusion too egregious an instance of human error to have any Divine sanction to it. Others accepted the teaching with varying degrees of consternation and perplexity but persevered with "all patience and faith," trusting that greater clarity would one day come. And, of course, far too many were untroubled, sharing in the same cultural prejudices and presuppositions that may have influenced the perpetuation of the practice. No simple formula resolves the tensions that do—and should—exist between faith in the principle of inspired leadership and personal responsibility to follow counsel without stifling conscience. Elder Dallin Oaks made a related point: "As a General Authority, it is my responsibility to preach general principles. When I do, I don't try to define all the exceptions. . . . I only teach the general rules. Whether an exception applies to you is your responsibility. You must work that out individually between you and the Lord."[21]

At the same time, it only compounds our consternation when we interpret the actions of Mormon leadership in the least, rather than most, generous way possible. One example pertains to the Church's handling of the Mormon past. Our history, as portrayed in manuals and curricular materials, has historically been edited to portray Mormons at their best and the world at its worst. Episodes and actions that reflect poorly on the Mormon people (like the Mountain Meadows Massacre) or create awkward questions (like Joseph Smith's plural marriages) were largely omitted or downplayed. Coming out of a legacy of bitter conflict, persecution, expulsion, and martyrdom, early Mormon historians felt no compunction about portraying the Mormon past as a black-and-white struggle between God's covenant people and gentile oppressors. The trauma and unrequited murder of Joseph and Hyrum in particular lingered long not just in collective but in personal memory.

A friend of the Smith family described the scene in the Mansion House when the bodies of the two victims of the mob were laid out following their return to Nauvoo: "I shall not attempt to discribe the scene that we have passed through. God forbid that I should ever witness another like unto it. I saw the lifeless corpses of our beloved brethren when they were brought to their almost distracted families. Yea I witnessed their tears, and groans, which was enough to rend the heart of an adamant."[22] Joseph F. Smith, Hyrum's son, was not yet six when he stood by his father's bullet-riddled body as part of that group of mourners. As an adult, Joseph F. would preside over the Church until 1918. His son, Joseph Fielding, who would have heard this account firsthand from his father, served as assistant Church historian from 1908 to 1921, and then as Church historian until 1970.

Doubtless such a past, coupled with a lingering sense of injustice and alienation, contributed to a protective disposition in Church history writing and archival access. The reforms initiated and then aborted under Leonard J. Arrington's professionalization of the department of Church History were renewed more successfully at the close of the twentieth century. Church resources are now being employed to explore and disseminate, rather than elide or suppress, a comprehensive history. From a frank and full account of the Mountain Meadows Massacre, to the complete record of Joseph Smith's journals, legal entanglements, and revelations (including every change, edit, or addition ever made), to the long unavailable Council of Fifty and Female Relief Society minutes, transparency and completeness have become the new norm.

For many of the Church's leadership, who have not been trained as professional historians, the still emerging details of early Mormon history may be as novel and unanticipated as they are to the lay membership. That polygamy ceased gradually rather than abruptly in 1890, that differing versions of the First Vision exist, that Joseph found a seerstone more congenial to his purposes than the Urim and Thummim—these and other peculiarities of the Mormon past are not closely guarded secrets gradually leaked out by a conspiring leadership, but products of historical investigation long known for the most part only to the specialists (and energetic amateurs) who had the time and expertise to delve into historical archives. That they are slow making their way into lesson manuals and Church history curricula is certainly true. That they are now coming to infuse Latter-day Saint websites and official publications—and will do so with increasing effectiveness—is equally apparent.

"Imperfect people are all God has ever had to work with," reminds Elder Jeffrey Holland. "That must be terribly frustrating to Him, but He deals with it. So should we."[23] Generosity with our own inept attempts to serve and minister to each other in a lay church, charity toward those in leadership who, as President Dieter Uchtdorf noted, have "said or done [things] that were not in harmony with our values, principles, or doctrine,"[24] and faith in Christ's Atonement that makes up the human deficit—these could be the balm of Gilead for which both wounded disciples and striving leaders seek.

CHAPTER 7

MORMONS AND MONOPOLIES:

HOLY PERSONS "YE KNOW NOT OF"

Read, sweet, how others strove,
Till we are stouter;
What they renounced,
Till we are less afraid;
How many times they bore the faithful witness,
Till we are helped
As if a kingdom cared.
Read then of faith
That shone above the fagot,
Clear strains of hymn
The river could not drown,
Brave names of men
And celestial women
Passed out of record
Into renown.

—EMILY DICKINSON[1]

The old Catholic Church is worth more than all.[2]

The language of Mormon culture, like that of most other cultures, is fraught with contradictions. All faiths have their intemperate zealots, and even the wisest and best men and women can say uninspired, ridiculous, and even reprehensible things. The religious scholar Krister Stendahl has suggested that in evaluating religions, it is only fair to characterize a faith group in terms of its best, not its worst, manifestations.[3] Generosity, historical context, and the filter of canonization all allow us to see the religious past more charitably as well as more accurately. Sometimes this principle is one that members need to apply to *our own* faith tradition. One example concerns the intemperate language often employed—especially in the early Latter-day Saint Church—to characterize other faith groups.

Many readers of Joseph Smith's First Vision account feel the sting of a wide-net rebuke, with its reference to the Christian creeds as "an abomination" in God's sight. Harsh to modern ears, however, Smith's language fits right into his cultural milieu. Religious discourse of prior ages was a vigorous and, by modern standards, shockingly abrasive and nasty hurly-burly of insults and slurs. Writers of the past probably felt the Jesus of the New Testament was a safe model to emulate: According to the scriptural record, Christ called His detractors evil, adulterers, whited sepulchers, hypocrites, snakes, and Satan spawn (children of "the devil").[4] And so it is no surprise that we should find Martin Luther calling Jews "venomous serpents" and full of the "devil's feces . . . which they wallow in like swine."[5] John Knox, father of the Scottish Reformation, called the Catholic Church a "blasphemous beast,"[6] and Calvin wrote that the Anabaptists were rightly condemned for their "ravings and slanders."[7]

In Smith's own day, one Mr. Edwards of Christ Church attacked Baptists as "notorious seducers" and "willful abettors of abominable errors."[8] The Methodists, wrote someone else in the early nineteenth century, were "anti-Christians" characterized by "insanity," "frantic ideas," and "anti-Christian" delusions.[9] An Anglican Bishop wrote that Methodists and Catholics were both victims of "depraved imaginations."[10] All this was comparatively tame. Dozens of books were at that time quoting Protestant authorities to the effect that Catholics were "not only filthy but also poisoned and venomed beasts," and worse.[11]

While Smith's language was typical of the era, the "abominations" he alluded to were not, contrary to general assumption, in reference to the Catholic creeds. Indeed, Smith felt it was the Protestant creeds that were the root of Christianity's most lamentable errors. The creedal formulation most attacked by early Mormon writers, and defended by their antagonists, had nothing to do with the Athanasian or Nicene controversies. It was the Protestant wording of the Anglican Thirty-Nine Articles (1563), largely incorporated into the Westminster Confession of Faith (1646), that Mormons criticized consistently. "There is but one only living and true God, everlasting, without body, parts, or passions [incorporeus, impartibilis, impassibilis]," held the document that was the theological basis for subsequent formulations of Presbyterians, Congregationalists, Baptists, and Methodists.[12] In fact, "the reigning theology of the country," noted a visiting German scholar in 1844, "is the theology of the Westminster Confession."[13]

The creedal "abomination" alluded to in Smith's First Vision was the clear suggestion of those creeds that God was an impersonal being, without a form, inaccessible and incomprehensible, unmoved by human suffering. As Edward Beecher, a Congregationalist minister, wrote in his own argument against the emotional sterility of such a creedal God, "If it is by the power of His emotions that God is to reign, then the denial of them is *the* great, radical, fundamental mode of destroying His reigning power, and of enthroning Satan in His stead. Nor is this all. Not only is this doctrine the centre of God's power, but it is also the centre of His greatness and glory."[14]

The colorful language of condemnation in Smith's account has contributed to a particularly pernicious myth that has had tragic influence on Mormon thinking. This is the notion that Mormonism has a monopoly on the truth, that other churches and traditions have nothing of value to contribute, and that the centuries between the death of the apostles and the events of 1820 were utterly blighted and devoid of truth. Some of those disaffected with the Church have even cited those perceptions as factors in their disaffection. One such person, in his farewell explanation, claimed that "Mormons believe that the church—Catholic, Orthodox, and Protestant visions alike—completely died," and quoted another dissident as saying, "The idea that God was sort of snoozing until 1820 now seems to me absurd."[15] Two points are crucial to make by way of comment here. First, some members may indeed harbor such unfortunate ideas. To that extent, the words of Stendahl are again relevant: no church should be judged by the regrettable opinions of the least enlightened. Second, both the Lord and leaders of The Church of Jesus Christ of Latter-day Saints have emphatically indicated a contrary perspective. In other words, the idea of Mormonism's monopoly and God's inaction during the pre-Restoration centuries would strike Joseph Smith and the likes of John Taylor as absurd as well.

If Joseph initially thought only Mormons had access to truth or goodness, he was abruptly corrected of his misperception a year into the Church's founding. In an 1831 revelation, the Lord told him that most of the world was under sin, "except those which I have reserved unto myself, holy men *that ye know not of*."[16] The words were a poignant indication that while Joseph might be a true prophet, the Lord's disciples were not limited to those who found themselves in the restored Church. In fact, the Lord directed one revelation to those who feared the restoration represented a condemnation of all Christian forms already present on the earth. The new church's organization did not, He said, threaten to annul "that which they have received." In fact, He declared that He acknowledged many people as already belonging to His church in 1829, even before the restored gospel took its present form under Joseph Smith's direction: "And for this cause have I said: If this generation harden not their hearts, I will establish my church among them. Now I do not say this to destroy my church, but I say this to build up my church; Therefore, whosoever belongeth to my church need not fear, for such shall inherit the kingdom of heaven."[17]

Another development reinforced Joseph's growing appreciation for a generous dispersal of God's influence beyond the reaches of a single institution. As he was working on the translation of the Book of Mormon in March 1829, he first learned of his role in a much larger mission to come; he was apparently to be involved in the expressed intention to "establish my church."[18] The mode or process was yet to be revealed. As Joseph revised that 1829 revelation for republication in 1835, he changed the wording considerably to reflect an apparently new understanding of what had happened to the original church. Even though priesthood authority and ordinances had been lost, truth had not departed the earth entirely, and

God had not abandoned His people to spiritual famine. The twelfth chapter of Revelation, which Joseph and most Protestants read as an allegory of the apostasy, notes emphatically that pressed by the forces of evil, the Lord's church is not taken from the earth; she retreats "into the wilderness," where "she hath a place *prepared of God.*" There, "*she is nourished,*" like Elisha in the cave, cared for by that God who is ever faithful.[19] Apparently moved by this insight, Joseph recast section 4 of the Book of Commandments to describe the Restoration as the Church's "coming forth . . . out of the wilderness."[20] Doctrines that had been peripheral would be made central. Teachings that had been preserved by the few would be made available to all. Smith apparently imbibed the lesson Jesus taught, that he who is truly "instructed in the kingdom of heaven" knows he must "[bring] forth out of his treasure things new and old."[21]

How did God nourish His people and keep the fires of truth burning when the gospel ordinances were no longer available in their fullness? It appears that when God lacked prophets, He spoke through poets and musicians, sages and simple men and women of faith and goodness. He spoke through Michelangelo's *Pietà* and Gerard Manley Hopkins's poetry and Bach's *St. Matthew's Passion.* He spoke through wise men such as the second-century Origen, who taught of our premortal existence in God's presence, of a God who felt our pain as His own, and of a Father's love so infinite that it would embrace the whole human family. He spoke through the fourteenth-century Julian of Norwich, who taught the necessity of sin and saw in Adam and Eve's fateful decision a bold step into mortality, not a catastrophic fall from grace. In vision, she learned that since the first parents, like all who leave the premortal realm, undertook their task out of love and "good wylle," they will be compensated for their pain and suffering, their fear and anxiety, to an extent "above that they should have had if they had not fallen."[22] And he spoke through the seventeenth-century poet Thomas Traherne, who celebrated the innocence of children against the almost universal chorus defending the destructive doctrine of original sin:

> But that which most I wonder at, which most
> I did esteem my bliss, which most I boast
> And ever shall enjoy, is that within
> I felt no stain nor spot of sin.
> No darkness then did overshade,
> But all within was pure and bright,
> No guilt did crush nor fear invade,
> But all my soul was full of light.[23]

God also spoke through Lady Anne Conway and Sarah Edwards and Edward Beecher and literally thousands of others who received ministrations of the Spirit that helped them maintain intact the most radiant truths of the gospel as the original institutional church fractured and fractured again. Meanwhile, through centuries of reform and turmoil, Catholics, in particular, kept alive the knowledge that the living and the dead are intimately connected, their condition and fates intimately intertwined. "You are as bad as the papists," said nineteenth-century critics of the Church, detecting a suspicious similarity between Mormon beliefs and the Catholic doctrine of purgatory. Rather than distance the practice from what contemporaries labeled an apostate papist teaching, the Mormon editor Thomas Ward responded: "We believe, that . . . [the Roman Catholic Church] has traces of many glorious principles that were once in the church of Christ, of which . . . the protestant world knows nothing."[24] In words that should shame those moderns who believe the medieval church was a spiritual wasteland, President John Taylor paid tribute to those holy ones of the past, counterparts of the holy ones Joseph was alerted to in his own day: "There were men in those dark ages who could commune with God, and who, by the power of faith, could draw aside the curtain of eternity and gaze upon the invisible world. . . . There were men who could gaze upon the face of God, have the ministering of angels, and unfold the future destinies of the world. If those were dark ages I pray God to give me a little darkness."[25] Brigham Young could be similarly generous in his conception of who would be found elect in the end: "I never passed John Wesley's church in London without stopping to look at it. Was he a good man? Yes; I suppose him to have been, by all accounts, as good as ever walked on this earth, according to his knowledge. Has he obtained a rest? Yes, and greater than ever entered into his mind to expect; and so have thousands of others of the various religious denominations."[26]

Those words of John Taylor and Brigham Young were entirely in the spirit of Joseph Smith's restorationism. If Mormons exude a sense of having a monopoly on an understanding of eternal things, or condemn the Dark Ages as being devoid of light and truth, they do so in ignorance of, not in conformity with, the work of Joseph and his associates. True, it was for Joseph to restore the knowledge of the saving and sealing ordinances, and to receive the priesthood keys to perform them. But Joseph also knew that, like the ruins of an ancient temple, "in broken fragments scattered, rent, and disjointed," beautiful remnants of the original church lay all about them, as "scattered fragments of Mormonism."[27]

A problem related to perceptions of Mormonism's monopoly on truth is the impression that Mormons claim a monopoly on salvation. It grows increasingly difficult to imagine that a body of a few million, in a world of seven billion, can really be God's only chosen people and heirs of salvation. That's because they aren't. One of the most unfortunate misperceptions about Mormonism is in this tragic irony: Joseph Smith's view is one of the most generous, liberal, and universalist conceptions of salvation in all Christendom. In section 49, when the Lord refers to "holy men" about whom Joseph knew nothing, and whom the Lord had reserved unto Himself, He is clearly indicating that Mormons do not have a monopoly on righteousness, truth, or God's approbation. That temple covenants may be made and kept here or hereafter, and the ordinances of salvation performed in person or vicariously, means our conception of His church should be as large and as generous as God's heart. Joseph's teachings suggest that the Church is best understood as a portal for the saved, not the reservoir of the righteous.

As a mighty God, our Heavenly Father has the capacity to save us all. As a fond father, He has the desire to do so. That is why, as Joseph taught, "God hath made a provision that *every* spirit can be ferretted out in that world" that has not deliberately and definitively chosen to resist a grace that is stronger than the cords of death.[28] The idea is certainly a generous one, and it flows naturally from the weeping God of Enoch, the God who has set His heart upon us. If some inconceivable few will persist in rejecting the course of eternal progress, they are "the only ones" who will be damned, taught Joseph Smith. "All the rest" of us will be rescued from the hell of our private torments and subsequent alienation from God.[29]

Both Brigham Young and Lorenzo Snow imbibed Smith's generous bent. Young preached, "Every faithful Methodist that has lived up to and faithfully fulfilled the requirements of his religion, . . . will have as great a heaven as he ever anticipated in the flesh, and far greater. Every Presbyterian, and every Quaker, and every Baptist, and every Roman Catholic member . . . that lives according to the best light they have, . . . will have and enjoy all they live for. . . . This is the situation of Christendom after death. You may go among the Pagans, or among all the nations there are . . . and if they have lived according to what they did possess, so they will receive hereafter. And will it be glory? you may inquire. Yes. Glory, glory, glory."[30]

Wilford Woodruff, in encouraging an all-encompassing project of genealogical research and family sealing back to Adam, justified it in terms of his vision of a wide-ranging salvation. "All who have died without a knowledge of this Gospel, who would have received it if they had been permitted to tarry, shall be heirs of the celestial kingdom. . . . So it will be with your fathers. There will be very few, if any, who will not accept the Gospel."[31] Lorenzo Snow concurred: "Very, very few of those who die without the Gospel will reject it on the other side of the veil."[32] Snow too believed God would persist in His salvific efforts until He succeeded. "The antediluvians rejected the word of God; but they were the sons and daughters of God, and . . . after twenty-five hundred years had passed away the Lord revealed Himself to them again and gave them another opportunity. Then they no doubt accepted. . . . The people of this generation may not receive our testimony here, but they will receive it at some future time, from us or from some other servants of God."[33]

J. Reuben Clark Jr. was of the same mind: "It is my belief that God will save all of His children that he can; and while, if we live unrighteously here, we shall not go to the other side in the same status, so to speak, as those who lived righteously; nevertheless, the unrighteous will have their chance, and in the eons of the eternities that are to follow, they, too, may climb to the destinies to which they who are righteous and serve God, have climbed."[34]

Perhaps the most important principle to keep in mind in considering our postmortal state is summed up best in this statement from George Q. Cannon, as quoted by President Henry B. Eyring to similar effect: "There is not one of us that He has not desired to save, and that He has not devised means to save."[35]

Sadly, not all Mormons have been inclined to celebrate such cosmic generosity. Brigham Young recorded that "when God revealed to Joseph Smith and Sidney Rigdon that there was a place prepared for all, according to the light they had received and their rejection of evil and practice of good, it was a great trial to many, and some apostatized because God was not going to send to everlasting punishment heathens and infants, but had a place of salvation, in due time, for all."[36] Like Jonah, some few want to see the burning of the tares. Like the resentful servant in the parable, a minority will always grumble that "these last have wrought but one hour, and thou hast made them equal unto us."[37]

Others, however, find incomparable solace in the hope that wayward spouses, rebellious children, or merely disinterested friends are not consigned to endless perdition. Elder Boyd K. Packer has said: "Save for the exception of the very few who defect to perdition, there is no habit, no addiction, no rebellion, no transgression, no crime exempted from the promise of complete forgiveness. That is the promise of the atonement of Christ. . . . This knowledge should be as comforting to the innocent as it is to the guilty [such as] parents who suffer unbearably for the mistakes of their wayward children and are losing hope."[38]

The generosity of such a vision necessarily spills over from the world's inhabitants to the legions of the dead. Even "the dead who repent will be redeemed, through obedience to the ordinances of the house of God," holds Mormon scripture.[39] One may doubt the efficacy of temple work, of rituals that purport to baptize the living on behalf of multitudes long dead. One Lutheran observer, however, expresses "holy envy" for the love manifest in putting into action a program that seeks to save all, living as well as dead.[40] "There is such a thing," G. K. Chesterton wrote, "as a small and cramped eternity. You may see it in many modern religions."[41] The heaven of Mormonism is no such place.

CHAPTER 8

SPIRITUALITY AND SELF-SUFFICIENCY:
FIND YOUR WATERING PLACE

·———·

Here are your waters and your watering place.
Drink and be whole again beyond confusion.

—ROBERT FROST[1]

Drink waters out of thine own cistern, and running waters out of thine own well.[2]

I t is ironic that a church characterized by one philosopher as having an "almost obsessive concern for free moral agency"[3] should be plagued from time to time by signs of spiritual dependency. One cause is suggested by a comment of Thomas Merton, the great Trappist mystic. When asked to diagnose the "leading spiritual disease of our time," he responded unexpectedly, "efficiency."[4] The Church is nothing if not efficient. Its ability to muster resources and respond to catastrophe is legendary. The speed of its communication network through visiting and home teaching chains is unparalleled. The genius of the Church's welfare program has been cited by U.S. presidents. It has tried and proven programs for gospel instruction of the young, activities for young women and young men, as well as organizations for men, women, and children. The Church doesn't just call its missionaries, it has autonomous training centers for them and provides instruction in more than fifty languages—with results that are the envy of language institutes everywhere. For members, there are classes for researching family history and for improving marriage relations. The Church even provides manuals for how families can have productive time together once a week. If there is a perceived need, the Church is there with a solution. Perhaps, one leader has chastened, at a cost:

"In recent years we might be compared to a team of doctors issuing prescriptions to cure or to immunize our members against spiritual diseases. Each time some moral or spiritual ailment was diagnosed, we have rushed to the pharmacy to concoct another remedy, encapsulate it as a program and send it out with pages of directions for use. . . . Over medication, over-programming is a critically serious problem."[5]

The catch with overprescribing is the dependency it creates. In the spiritual realm, it is easy for Mormons to grow accustomed to viewing their weekly meetings not just as opportunities to serve and renew covenants but as their primary sources of spiritual nourishment. But as both Robert Frost and the author of Proverbs knew, spiritual strength requires finding one's own well from which to drink. We should recognize, first, that we are responsible for our own spiritual diet, and second, that sources of inspiration are sprinkled indiscriminately throughout time and place. Mormons should feel empowered and inspired to fill our own wells with nourishing waters. A nineteenth-century historian of Christianity advocated the need "to search out the real Church from age to age, . . . indeed a work of much labour and difficulty. . . . The ore is precious, but it must be extracted from incredible heaps of Ecclesiastical rubbish."[6]

Following such advice, the poet Samuel Taylor Coleridge wrote movingly of the gratitude he felt to those numerous fonts of inspiration who had steered him through his own faith journey. Having in mind the great Christian mystics and holy men George Fox, Jacob Böhme, and William Law, he wrote of "the feeling of gratitude, which I cherish towards these men." He said their "writings acted in no slight degree to prevent my mind from being imprisoned within the outline of any single dogmatic system. They contributed to keep alive the heart in the head, gave me an indistinct, yet stirring and working presentiment" of "some root to which I had not penetrated. . . . They were always a pillar of fire throughout the night, during my wanderings through the wilderness of doubt, and enabled me to skirt, without crossing, the sandy deserts of utter unbelief."[7]

Doing likewise, as Mormon disciples of Christ we might see ourselves as participating in a larger community than the institutional church. The great Reformer John Calvin contrasted the invisible church, consisting of "the elect who have existed from the beginning of the world," with "the whole body of mankind scattered throughout the world, who profess to worship one God and Christ."[8] Böhme spoke of the *Kirche ohne Mauer* (church without walls) as a place where "all rejoice to have the one mother [Sophia or Wisdom]" and live in mutual love and support.[9] Are these not Protestant formulations of the truth alluded to in latter-day scriptures, that the larger community of Christ's saints are drawn from many traditions? The Lord calls the larger, transhistorical church of His elect "an innumerable company of angels, . . . the general assembly and church of Enoch, and of the Firstborn."[10] The expansive vision of that church was laid out even earlier, in an 1830 revelation wherein Christ promised one day to "drink of the fruit of the vine" with figures from Adam to Abraham to Elijah to Moroni to Peter—in fact, with "all those whom my Father hath given me out of the world."[11] That seems to reinforce the import of the scripture quoted in the last chapter: "I will establish my church among them. Now I do not say this to destroy my church, but I say this to build up my church; Therefore, whosoever belongeth to my church need not fear."[12]

There is solace and kinship to be found in a shared discipleship faithful Latter-day Saints feel with a larger community of those who choose to love and follow God. The injunction to seek wisdom "out of the best books," along with the Lord's reproof that "because that ye have a Bible [and other scriptures] ye need not suppose that it contains all my words," encourage a receptivity to the larger world of beauty and goodness and inspiration that God has cultivated.[13] As George MacDonald wrote, "to the man who would live throughout the whole divine form of his being, not confining himself to one broken corner of the kingdom, . . . a thousand questions will arise to which the Bible does not even allude. . . . Sad, indeed, would the whole matter be, if the Bible told us *everything* God meant us to believe."[14]

The challenge, then, and the enticing opportunity, is to find a pattern of devotion and nourishment that extends beyond the confines of a Sunday curriculum, one that constitutes our private life of discipleship. ("Ah Lord! Be thou in all our being; as not in the Sundays of our time alone," prayed MacDonald.)[15] For while the established Church provides a framework of service, an occasion for community, and a vehicle for saving ordinances, it is in the secret chambers of our private temples that we must have ultimate recourse to the inspiration and revelation that guide our discipleship. In establishing this pattern, this private watering place, we can feed on those spiritual nutrients that most inspire and sustain us. "The great heresy of the Church of the present day," added MacDonald, referring to the Christian community generally, "is unbelief in this Spirit. The mass of the Church does not believe that the Spirit has a revelation for every man individually—a revelation as different from the revelation of the Bible, as the food in the moment of passing into living brain and nerve differs from the bread and meat."[16]

Wells may be replenished as we drink liberally from the words of poets, writers, theologians, and essayists representing a host of cultures and traditions. Gospel insights and an enriched understanding of discipleship, together with a bond of sisterhood and brotherhood across time and place, can lift us out of the mundane, the familiar, and the narrow neighborhood of our own spiritual journeys. Ironically, in other words, it is in filling the private wells of our faith that we find an unexpected camaraderie with other disciples, in a circle that far transcends the confines of our meetinghouse.

Joseph Smith owned books by Calvinist preachers, lectures on Universalism, a Catholic prayer book, meditations by the Reverend James Hervey, and five volumes of Walter Scott's poetry.[17] David O. McKay could reportedly quote 1,000 poems from memory, and he referred to literary masters as "minor prophets."[18] Spencer W. Kimball loved literature and quoted liberally from great authors, as well as penning his own poetry ("Young love is beautiful to contemplate/ But old love is the finished tapestry/Stretched out from oaken floors to heaven's gate . . .").[19] Brigham Young set a standard still too little appreciated when he declared that "Our religion takes within its wide embrace not only things of heaven, but also things of earth. It circumscribes all art, science, and literature."[20]

Reading one day a sermon from the fourth-century Church Father Gregory of Nazianzus, we were struck by the love and piety manifest in this figure from the ancient past. He wrote feelingly of the same Christ we worship:

> Jesus Who Chose The Fishermen, Himself also useth a net, and changeth place for place. Why? Not only that He may gain more of those who love God by His visitation; but also, as it seems to me, that He may hallow more places. . . . He is made a Fisherman; He condescendeth to all; He casteth the net; He endureth all things, that He may draw up the fish from the depths, that is, Man who is swimming in the unsettled and bitter waves of life. . . . He teacheth, now on a mountain; now He discourseth on a plain; now He passeth over into a ship; now He rebuketh the surges. And perhaps He goes to sleep, in order that He may bless sleep also; perhaps He is tired that He may hallow weariness also; perhaps He weeps that He may make tears blessed.[21]

Surely there is profit to be gained in recognizing the devotion of the venerable Gregory, a love and holy sympathy for Christ that had the power to lead him to the font of wisdom. Surely we can recognize a bond we share with him and all those committed to defending the Good, the True, and the Beautiful and find inspiration in their discipleship. Surely we can feel at home, not just in our Mormon community of aspiring saints, but in the larger church without walls, peopled by the devout, the holy, and the exemplary from myriad times and traditions.

Such a path requires self-direction. One friend noted her own recommitment to "deliberately dive into a more proactive, self-created path for [her] spirituality."[22] The Church is a place to worship, to serve others, to learn to get along with people we might not choose as neighbors or family, and to find kinship with a large and timeless community of disciples. It is a workshop for the soul. But ultimately, we are responsible for our own life of discipleship, for finding spiritual nourishment in our own sacred spaces. At the same time, we are part of the body of Christ—and we can influence the collective only if we are part of it. As an outspoken president once noted, "It is not the critic who counts; not the man who points out how the strong man stumbles, or where the doer of deeds could have done them better. The credit belongs to the man who is actually in the arena."[23]

Mere months after the organization of the Church, Joseph was told that this, the last work of the Lord, was to be created "first temporal[ly], and secondly spiritual[ly]."[24] One way to read this is as a reminder that the formal, institutional parameters of the New Jerusalem are easy to put in place. The organizational structure, the blueprints for temples and plats for Zion came readily enough. Forging a people sufficiently sanctified to constitute the people of Zion is another matter entirely. According to the sequence alluded to by the revelation above, we would expect the spiritual qualities of Church members to lag behind the temporal templates—the buildings and programs—within which we work out our salvation. That sequence should further forewarn us of two attitudinal shifts that may be required as we labor to build Zion together: a spirit of patience and one of participation.

PATIENCE

Trials of faith seldom arise from core Mormon beliefs; few struggle with commitment because their God is too benevolent, His plan too generous, the heaven we anticipate too rich in relationships and love. Doctrines, however, no matter how pure, do not exist in a vacuum. We encounter them through teachings, programs, manuals, personal interactions, and institutional forms and practices. And in the process, we occasionally find the pure gospel entangled with unfortunate ideas, pharisaical behavior, legalistic thinking, judgmentalism, and rules based more on tradition than inspiration. Those, of course, are the fruits of culture—a primarily western American Mormon culture almost two centuries in the making. They are not the gospel itself. But the complaint that culture, not the gospel, is the problem, is not entirely satisfactory. Our experience of the gospel is inescapably mediated by, conditioned by, culture. We would suggest a more fruitful perspective.

In Salt Lake's old Thirteenth Ward, Bishop Edwin D. Woolley frequently found himself at odds with President Brigham Young. On a certain occasion, as they ended one such fractious encounter, Young had a final parting remark: "Now, Bishop Woolley, I guess you will go off and apostatize." To which the bishop rejoined, "If this were your church, President Young, I would be tempted to do so. But this is just as much my church as it is yours, and why should I apostatize from my own church?"[25] That sense of ownership, or, better, of full and equal membership in the body of Christ, was Bishop Woolley's salvation. He wisely realized, as not all do, that forsaking the Church out of hurt or frustration would be as unprofitable as any other form of misdirected energy. It would make as much sense, in one author's words, as "drinking rat poison and waiting for the rat to die."[26] In Nephi's less colorful query, "Why should I give way . . . , that the evil one have place in my heart to destroy my peace and afflict my soul?"[27] Why so willingly give up our spiritual home to emotional termites?

PARTICIPATION

We have all bemoaned the traffic congestion at rush hour, or the heavily populated mountain path where we had hoped to find solitude. We forget that from the perspective of the other travelers—and from any objective point of view—*we* are the problem we bewail. *We* are part of the gawking crowds at the overlook, *we* are an impediment to other anxious shoppers in the checkout line, *we* are the head and shoulders blocking a perfect view from the moviegoer behind us. Just as we are a part of the Mormon culture we lament. If we allow ourselves to be co-opted by practices or attitudes we deplore, we share in the collective guilt.

The pressure to conform to what we see as a dominant cultural orthodoxy is often more imagined than real. A silent majority may be more receptive than we realize to our own yearnings for greater authenticity, honesty, originality, and individualism. Brigham Young was. "I am not a stereotyped Latter-day Saint," he said, "and do not believe in the doctrine. . . . Away with stereotyped 'Mormons'!"[28] Such pressures to fit in, to keep silent in the face of dominant perspectives and attitudes and understandings, can seem a daunting specter. This is especially true in the case of those who, harboring doubts or uncertainties, feel marginalized by Mormonism's pervasive rhetoric of certainty. Yet, some have ventured to test the perceived cultural norms—and found the experiment rewarding. One young woman who felt marginalized by the certainty and expressions of conviction in every testimony meeting decided on one fast Sunday to speak out from her silent, self-imposed exile. This is her testimony:

> This last fast Sunday before the service began my bishop
> came and sat next to me for a moment to [share some of

his concerns about my spiritual well-being]. . . . So as I sat there during the sacrament and reflected on what had just happened I realized that I had never given my bishop the opportunity to get to know me or understand my frame of mind. I have been guarded and aloof in every interaction I have ever had with him. . . . I have never told anyone in my ward anything about my thoughts and feelings and I have kept myself a safe distance from personal interaction because I have been afraid of the judgment and marginalization that might occur should they discover my true feelings about things. I knew that things had to change if I am to find a way to be a happy part of this church. I need to be honest with myself and others in a way that is positive for everyone involved. I need to live by faith in God and not by fear of men.

So, I decided to bear my testimony. Or more accurately, my non-testimony. I said that as a child I feared that there was no God, that I pushed that down and that it had persisted always in those deepest places of fear. I spoke of my constant devotion to Christ and God during my adolescence despite the fear; that it wasn't until my mission that I experienced my first real question about the historical narrative we tell. And I told of how I always spoke the language of "I know" believing that the language made things right. I then said that after I married I encountered the fear again and decided to face it and look at it from all sides. So I began to ask all the questions in my mind and study and search them out. For ten years I have slowly waded through the doubts and questions of my intellect. . . . In the end I have come to one simple truth: we choose. We choose what we will believe in and live by. We choose how we will behave and what we will hope for. I then bore testimony that I know that when I follow Christ's teachings I have a better marriage. I know that when I serve and love others I am a happier person. I know that when I focus on love I form lasting deep relationships with others. I know that when I read scriptures in the morning with my daughter, she and I are happier together and more peaceful in our relationship. I do not know that the Church is true. I do not know that there is a God but I hope there is. I hope that the feelings of love and comfort and inspiration that would indicate that there is a loving God are not just brain chemicals and biology and psychology, but that they are evidences of Him. I hope that when we die we go home to loving Heavenly Parents. . . . And then I closed. I said all this with my bishop and stake president sitting behind me and all my ward listening. And it felt wonderful. The days since have been filled with response enough. People have been concerned and kind and loving. They don't fully understand the language I used or the story I told and they are coming from a place of reclamation, but they have been loving. And love is something that will build a bridge between us. So I am content. But more importantly I feel free.

This member exemplified the counsel of Elder Jeffrey Holland, "I am not asking you to pretend to faith you do not have. I am asking you to be true to the faith you do have."[29] It is important to recognize, as well, that hostility shown toward our doubts is often a sign of fear rather than intolerance. Those who express uncertainties can elicit discomfort from those experiencing their own secret struggles and confusion from those who do not struggle in the same way.

Certainly it is in the nature of institutions to homogenize disparities, to stifle individualism. But the Creator God of Genesis is a Being who revels in distinctions, difference, and variation, an Artificer who separated man from woman as surely as He severed earth from sky. And love is the spark that fires across the chasm of difference, not the plane of sameness. This is as true of Zion as it is of marriage. The poet Coventry Patmore wrote that the bonds that unite us in community consist "not in similarity, but in dissimilarity; the happiness of love, in which alone happiness resid[es] . . . not in unison, but conjunction, which can only be between spiritual dissimilars."[30]

This is why the body of Christ needs its full complement of members—the devout, the wayward, the uncomfortable, the struggling. "It does not mean that a man is not good because he errs in doctrine," Joseph said of a Mormon rebuked by others for his preaching. "It feels so good not to be trammeled."[31] This is the spirit in which one Church leader recently noted that not only unique backgrounds but "unique talents and perspectives" and "diversity of persons and peoples" are "a strength of this Church."[32]

CHAPTER 9

THE TOO-TENDER HEART:

RETHINKING BEING "OVERCOME WITH EVIL"

•——————•

O yet we trust that somehow good
Will be the final goal of ill,
To pangs of nature, sins of will,
Defects of doubt, taints of blood; . . .

That not a worm is cloven in vain;
That not a moth with vain desire
Is shrivell'd in a fruitless fire,
Or but subserves another's gain.

Behold, we know not anything;
I can but trust that good shall fall
At last—far off—at last, to all,
And every winter change to spring.

So runs my dream; but what am I?
An infant crying in the night:
An infant crying for the light:
And with no language but a cry.

—ALFRED, LORD TENNYSON[1]

Instead of explaining our suffering, God shares it.[2]

Mormonism may not have a satisfactory, full explanation for the unspeakable evil to which humans have been, and always will be, subjected in this mortal crucible. The worst depravities inflicted on suffering innocence may be the unstoppable consequences of a world predicated on the foundation of unfettered moral agency. As C. S. Lewis wrote, "Either something or nothing must depend on individual choices. And if something, who could set bounds to it?"[3] That is why many have concluded, along with the novelist Norman Mailer, that the specter of colossal human pain requires no God, a perverse God, or a God self-limited by human freedom. "If God is good, then He is not all powerful. If God is all powerful, then He is not all good. I am a disbeliever in the omnipotence of God because of the Holocaust. But for thirty-five years or so, I have been believing that He is doing the best He can."[4]

That recognition, of course, still leaves us to contend with the likes of typhoons, the plague, and birth defects. Those who have suffered tragedy, personally or vicariously, know that the sacrilege of glib consolation is worse than silence. (Job's friends knew that too, at least initially, and silently mourned for seven days in the presence of his suffering.) Trusting that suffering is sanctifying is of little use in the white heat of personal anguish. It is more helpful in such circumstances to validate real pain than to try to smooth over it. One aspect of Mormon thought does that in sobering terms.

Interestingly, it was the Congregationalist minister Edward Beecher who best articulated one of the most unique aspects of Mormon doctrine. A vigorous proponent of belief in human preexistence, he also accepted the scriptural account of a defection in the premortal ranks—what Mormons call "the war in heaven." This is how he understood the reason, in words strikingly consistent with Latter-day Saint understanding. "From pleasure, of course, there was no temptation to revolt; but from a discipline of suffering, such as they needed to fit them to be the founders of the universe with God, they could be tempted to revolt."[5] Mormons typically cast the war in heaven as a contest between freedom and coercion, risk and salvational assurance. Beecher's view is no different. He simply recognizes that freedom is the freedom to err, which is inseparably connected to risk: the risk of pain and loss.

What is particularly sobering about Beecher's observation is the reasonable likelihood to which he points us that human suffering, in which we are at present either immersed or of which we stand witness, and of which we were doubtless forewarned in detail, was shocking enough—daunting enough—to dissuade billions upon billions of the premortal hosts, our spiritual siblings, from venturing forth into mortality. The Mormon conception of the war in heaven has ill served us in the simplistic, caricatured forms it so often takes. More must have been involved than simple choice between freedom and coercion. Depriving the human family of agency and accountability could only have been tempting to sons and daughters of God if the alternative were unthinkably terrible. The most reasonable explanation of heavenly division was not over some vague risk of failure that we bravely accepted while others cravenly retreated.

More likely, as Beecher argued, was the very real, vivid, inevitable pageant of warfare, genocide, infant mortality, an almost universal anguish for sin and personal bereavement that, once unfolded to our eyes in celestial councils, threatened to derail the entire plan, drawing away a third of the heavenly hosts.

Believing this to be what transpired those eons ago offers no easy comfort. But perhaps it may prompt us to consider that human misery is not to be dismissed with platitudes, accounted mere weakness of faith, or resolved with just the right theodicy, or philosophy of human suffering. The mythic memory of those events and projected costs might serve to endow Paul's words with new meaning: "Be not overcome of evil."[6] Paul's fear may have been, not that we as disciples would fall prey to the *allure* of evil, but that as compassionate spectators we would fall prey to the *weight* of evil, and turn to despair, hopelessness, or bitterness. This is why Julian of Norwich so compassionately counseled, "For it is [Satan's] meaning to make us so heavy and so sorry in this that we should forget the blessed beholding of our everlasting friend."[7]

One of the greatest meditations on the problem of human evil occurs in Fyodor Dostoevsky's masterpiece *The Brothers Karamazov*. In the chapter "Rebellion," the nihilist Ivan chronicles to his brother, the gentle-souled novitiate priest Alyosha, the horrific suffering of young children in graphic and agonizing detail. He describes, in scenes taken from contemporary accounts, a little girl tortured and brutalized by cruel parents and a young boy torn apart by the dogs of a sadistic estate owner. In the novel's most devastating scene, he then manages to elicit from the now pained and shattered Alyosha the admission that he cannot countenance that moral universe to which he has devoted his life. "Tell me frankly, I appeal to you—answer me," Ivan cruelly prods his brother, "imagine that it is you yourself who are erecting the edifice of human destiny with the aim of making men happy in the end, of giving them peace and contentment at last, but that it is absolutely necessary, and indeed quite inevitable, to torture to death only one tiny creature. . . . Would you consent to be the architect on those conditions? Tell me and do not lie!" And Alyosha responds with a barely audible whisper, "No, I wouldn't."[8]

Like Milton's Adam after the Fall, love for the other has cost Alyosha his loyalty to God. Rather than approve a world marred by the tears of innocent children, he denies the value and meaning of the entire plan of creation. He has now apparently joined his antagonist brother in the ultimate gesture of the most complete repudiation; as Ivan has said moments earlier, "It's not God that I don't accept, Alyosha, only I most respectfully return him the ticket."[9] We too may decide the cost of innocent suffering is too high. Impotence in the face of another's pain is the greatest of all suffering, as anyone knows whose love for another—the daughter in depression, the innocent children read about in the school shooting—has exacted sleepless nights, broken hearts, and rage against the universe. But perhaps raging against the universe—even against God—is not the sin some people think it to be.

Reb Dovid Din was sought out in Jerusalem by a man who was suffering a crisis of belief. . . . He listened and listened to the man, who ranted and raved for hours. At last he said to him: "Why are you so angry with God?" . . . Then Reb Dovid stood up and told the man to follow him. He led him to the Wailing Wall, away from the place where people pray to the site of the ruins of the Temple. When they reached that place, Reb Dovid told him that it was time to express all the anger he felt toward God. Then, for more than an hour, the man struck the wall of the Kotel with his hands and screamed his heart out. After that he began to cry and could not stop crying, and little by little his cries became sobs that turned into prayers. And that is how Reb Dovid Din taught him how to pray.[10]

Surely God is not so fragile, so lacking in empathy, that He would take offense at our incredulity or our anger in the face of the world's wounds. For our pain is already His. As a theologian who lost his own son wrote, "Through our tears, we see the tears of God." And believing, as Mormons do, that God is the infinitely suffering God of Enoch, not the "impassive, unresponsive" God "portrayed by the classical theologians," this writer added a poignant possibility: "It is said of God that no one can behold His face and live. I always thought this meant that no one could behold His splendor and live. . . . Perhaps it meant that no one could see His sorrow and live."[11]

Those entering into the baptismal covenant pledge not just to comfort those who are downcast, but to share in their suffering—to "mourn with those that mourn."[12] We are called, in other words, to "be open to the wounds of the world," to "be in agony over humanity's agony."[13] As the philosopher Nicholas Wolterstorff has written, "We all suffer. For we all prize and love; and in this present existence of ours, prizing and loving yield suffering. Love in our world is suffering love. Some do not suffer much, though, for they do not love much. Suffering is for the loving."[14]

This is probably not what we anticipated. We expect the gospel to make us happy. From our youth we are taught that God answers prayers, that all blessings can be anticipated as a direct and predictable result of a corresponding commandment, that obedience brings happiness. The empathy shown by Brigham Young is striking: "To profess to be a Saint, and not enjoy the spirit of it, tries every fiber of the heart, and is one of the most painful experiences that man can suffer."[15] He realized that then, as now, thousands of Saints were paying the high price of discipleship and asking, "Where is the joy?" And he knew the question was born in agony and bewilderment. Life can be excruciating at the worst of times, and unhappy at the best. To live without God in the world, without hopes or expectations, without spiritual balm or religious faith, is trying. To live a life of discipleship and then feel hopes dashed and expectations unfulfilled, the balm ineffective and the faith devoid of fruit, is to compound the pain with devastating disappointment and heart-ache. False hope seems worse than none; better to know one is alone in the sea than to wait for the rescue that never comes. When devotion to prayer, scripture study, and obedience do not suffice, we might turn to patience, remembering, solace in the fellowship of the desolate, and hope.

In Lehi's nighttime vision, wherein events are compressed into moments, he recorded his striking impression that he "traveled for the space of many hours in darkness" before he came to the "large and spacious field."[16] Joseph's prayers in Kirtland were months in the answering, though lives hung in the balance. Simeon spent an entire lifetime "waiting for the consolation of Israel" and beheld the infant Jesus only at life's twilight. So it was with the temple proph-etess Anna, likewise rewarded when only upon reaching "great age" did she see the awaited Christ child.[17] Patience does not mean to wait apathetically and dejectedly, but to anticipate actively on the basis of what we hope to be true and what we know to be true; and what we know, we must remember.

Remembering can be the highest form of devotion. To remem-ber is to rescue the sacred from the vacuum of oblivion. To remember Christ's sacrifice every Sunday at the sacrament table is to say "no" to the ravages of time—to refuse to allow his supernal sacrifice to be just another datum in the catalogue of what is past. To remember past blessings is to give continuing recognition of the gift and to reconfirm the relationship to the Giver as one that persists in the here and now. Few—very few—are entirely bereft of at least one solace-giving memory: a childhood prayer answered, a testimony borne long ago, a fleeting moment of perfect peace.

Our present, of course, is shaped by our past. We are in many ways its product. But at the same time, we tend to reinterpret the past on the basis of the present. We are creatures of the moment, so, rather than remember, we reconstruct what once we knew in the light of present uncertainty or loss, which can all too easily over-whelm what we once held as true and real. All too often we forget the gentle impressions we felt, the calm soothing of troubled hearts and minds, or even greater manifestations of divine love. The in-tuitive poet Mary Oliver suggests that after Christ's calming of the stormy sea, the passage of everyday life enveloped again the doubt-ful disciples, and swallowed up the memory of

> how the wind tore at the sails
> before he rose and talked to it—[18]

It is useful at such moments of doubt, if we can't exercise faith in God, to exercise faith in ourselves. We can trust that it was a good and trustworthy self that once knew certain things to be true—and may one day again. As the poet wrote, "whatsoever from one place doth fall,/ Is with the tide unto another brought:/ For there is nothing lost, that may be found, if sought."[19] At the same time, remembering rather than experiencing moves us toward greater independence and insulates us from the vicissitudes of the moment. Brigham Young thought God's intention was to make us as independent in our sphere as He is in His. Such independence may require that we learn to act on the basis of what drives us from within, rather than what acts upon us from without. It may be for this reason that the heavens close from time to time, to give us room for self-direction. "This is the place where every man com-mences to acquire the germ of the independence that is enjoyed in the heavens," Young said.[20] Which may explain why the Saints rejoiced in a Pentecostal day in Kirtland's temple, but were met with silence in Nauvoo. Silence—and their memories of Kirtland. One can see the Lord gently tutoring us to replace immediacy with memory in section 6 of the Doctrine and Covenants, when He says to Oliver, "If you desire a further witness, cast your mind upon the night that you cried unto me in your heart, that you might know concerning the truth of these things. Did I not speak peace to your mind concerning the matter? What greater witness can you have than from God?"[21]

C. S. Lewis wrote that "sooner or later [God] withdraws, if not in fact, at least from their conscious experience, all those supports and incentives. He leaves the creature to stand up on its own legs. . . . It is during such trough periods, much more than during the peak periods, that it is growing into the sort of creature He wants it to be." This is because "He wants servants who can finally become sons [and daughters]."[22] That may simply be, unavoidably, a wrenching process of spiritual abandonment such as Eve and Adam felt in their expulsion from God's presence, or we all must have felt upon leaving of our premortal estate. Perhaps this feeling of desolation was entailed in Joseph's remark that in our quest for understanding, we "must search into and contemplate the darkest abyss."[23] Perhaps many of us will never find God by calling out His name at the entrance to the cave; we must enter its depths.

And for those of us who despair that we have never heard so much as a whisper, we can be still and remember that we have known the goodness of love, the rightness of virtue, the nobility of kindness and faithfulness—and ask, can we not perceive in such moments the handwriting of God on our hearts and minds? If all else fails, we may find solace in what we might call the fellowship of the desolate. With Mother Teresa, who lived in spiritual wilderness for decades, describing

> this terrible sense of loss—this untold darkness—this lone-liness—this continual longing for God—which gives me that pain deep down in my heart.—Darkness is such that I really do not see—neither with my mind nor with my reason.—The place of God in my soul is blank.—There is no God in me.—When the pain of longing is so great—I just long and long for God and then it is that I feel—He does not want me—He is not there.— . . . God does not want

me.—Sometimes—I just hear my own heart cry out—"My God" and nothing else comes. The torture and pain I can't explain.[24]

Or with Julian of Norwich, who wrote years after her epiphanies, "For we be as barren and as dry oft times after our prayers as we were before. . . . For thus have I felt myself."[25] Or with the magnificent Jesuit poet Gerard Manley Hopkins, who poured out his soul in achingly beautiful lament:

> I wake and feel the fell of dark, not day.
> What hours, O what black hours we have spent
> This night! what sights you, heart, saw; ways you went!
> And more must, in yet longer light's delay.
> With witness I speak this. But where I say
> Hours I mean years, mean life. . . . [26]

There is gentle pleading, and no reprimand, in the prophet's counsel: "Only . . . keep thy soul diligently, lest thou forget the things which thine eyes have seen, and lest they depart from thy heart all the days of thy life."[27]

CHAPTER 10

OF SILENCE AND SOLITUDE:

"SPEAK, LORD, FOR THY SERVANT HEARETH"

—————•—————

I've listened: and all the sounds I heard
Were music,—wind, and stream, and bird.
With youth who sang from hill to hill
I've listened: my heart is hungry still.

I've looked: the morning world was green;
Bright roofs and towers of town I've seen;
And stars, wheeling through wingless night.
I've looked: and my soul yet longs for light.

I've thought: but in my sense survives
Only the impulse of those lives
That were my making. Hear me say
"I've thought!"—and darkness hides my day.

—SIEGFRIED SASSOON[1]

And what were thou, and earth, and stars, and sea,
If to the human mind's imaginings
Silence and solitude were vacancy?[2]

There are many kinds of silence, and not all signify absence, or vacancy. There is the stuttering awkwardness of non-response, as when a marriage proposal elicits panicky shock rather than the rapturous "yes" one hoped for. There is the silence of evasion, as when the father's query, "You didn't put your brother in the clothes dryer, did you?" is met with a frozen stare. Those moments of silence are but temporary ebbs before the flow of meaning rushes in to fill the space.

There is the still echo of absence, as when William Wordsworth turned to share a sudden joy with three-year-old Catherine—only to remember his beloved daughter was not at her accustomed place beside him on their walk, but "deep buried in the silent tomb."[3] Or when a grieving Phineas Hodson mourned the wife "who now hears not when he calls."[4] Those moments of silence are but a response painfully postponed.

Then again, some words that meet with silence are like what Gerard Manley Hopkins called, "Dead letters sent to dearest him that lives, alas, away."[5] Back in the days when lovers, college students, and frustrated customers still put pen to old-fashioned paper and handwrote their letters, some of those missives ended up in the dead-letter section of the post office. The address could be wrong, the recipient could be dead or moved on, or—in the case of those fleeing alimony or accountability—the address was a non-starter that described a phony person or a phony place. The poet Hopkins found times in his life when his prayers uttered in agony of soul were like those dead letters. The God he knew and loved was suddenly, for whatever reason, absent or unresponsive. Mother Teresa lamented, "I am told God lives in me and yet the reality of darkness and coldness and emptiness is so great that nothing touches my soul. . . . Heaven from every side is closed."[6]

That was the silence Joseph Smith himself knew at one of the most trying moments of his life and ministry. In the fall of 1830, the Zion of prophecy had been located and established in Jackson County, Missouri. The land was consecrated for the gathering of the faithful on August 2, 1831. The next day, a site was dedicated and corner markers laid for the Independence Temple. Thousands of converts poured in in response to the Prophet's call. Late in June 1833, the Prophet sent a plat for the building of the New Jerusalem, to accommodate fifteen to twenty thousand people, with sites for twenty-four temples anticipated. The heavens were open, the gospel was spreading abroad, Christ's return was imminent, and Joseph and his people were the envy of angels in heaven and "prophets, priests and kings" long dead, who "have looked forward with joyful anticipation to the day in which we live; and fired with heavenly and joyful anticipations they have sung and written and prophesied of this our day; but they died without the sight; we are the favored people that God has made choice of to bring about the Latter-day glory."[7]

Abruptly the dream turned to nightmare. In July, a mob struck, destroying the Church print shop and other property. Bishop Edward Partridge was tarred and feathered, and the residents were forced to sign an agreement of mass exile. The hopeful thousands were on the point of expulsion from their "land of peace," "city of refuge," and "place of safety for the saints of the Most High God." Hearing the shocking news, Smith penned an epistle to his distant flock.

> 18 August
> Dear Brotheren
>
> in fellowship and love towards you and with a broken heart . . . I take the pen to address you but I know not what to say. . . . My heart feints within me and I feel to exclaim O Lord let the desire of my heart be felt and realized this moment. . . . I verily know that [Christ] will speedily deliver Zion for I have his immutable covenant that this shall be the case but god is pleased to keep it hid from mine eyes.

At this moment, Joseph was a thousand miles away in Kirtland, Ohio, beset by his own enemies and conspirators. The distance and impotence of his predicament were unbearable: "never at any time have I felt as I now feel that pure love for you my Brotheren the wormth and Zeal for your safety that we can scarcely hold our spirits but wisdom I trust will keep us from madness and desperation."[8] Three months later, Joseph had received no heavenly insight into the dilemma. "How far [the mobs] will be suffered to execute their threats we know not," he wrote a convert.[9]

The situation turned even more tragic. Beatings, burnings, and destruction forced the Saints onto the unsheltered banks of the Missouri River ahead of the imposed deadline. As prophet and leader of his people, responsible for the deaths and suffering now unfolding, Joseph certainly felt he had a right as never before to a revelation clarifying the situation and giving him inspired direction. But the heavens were silent. Such answers, he lamented, "I cannot learn from any communication by the spirit to me." Of the reasons for their continuing plight, he added, "I am ignorant and the Lord will not show me." His prayers went up "to God day and night," with not only his peace of mind at stake but the life and death and welfare of hundreds. Yet all he could do was weep on their behalf, as silence met his anguished appeals.[10]

It is also possible that God's answers are sometimes too indirect, too oblique, for us to recognize because we are looking for something more palpable. During a relative's interview upon completing his mission, his president asked if the elder had anything remaining on his mind. "Yes," he said. "You promised us as new missionaries we could have, upon completion, the spiritual witness that our sacrifice was accepted of the Lord. I have prayed and fasted and worked earnestly for such a confirmation, and I have felt nothing. The heavens have been utterly silent."

The president heard these words with something close to weariness. "How do you feel about your mission?" he asked.

"I feel great," the missionary answered. "I have loved the people and the work. I go home knowing I did my best, and feel happy about my two years of service."

"And you don't think those feelings are an answer to your prayers? Your problem is you wanted something more dramatic to consume upon your lusts," the president concluded.

The president's language may have been a little harsh, but the point here is that we often, even unknowingly, impose expectations and preconditions on the kind of answer we anticipate. We want a discernible voice—though scriptures note such occurrences infrequently. We wait for a burning in the bosom—though that scriptural allusion was in reference to the gift of translation, not prayer.[11] Joseph admonished patience and practice in recognizing God's voice. "He that can mark the power of Omnipotence inscribed upon the heavens, can also see His own hand-writing in the sacred volume; and he who reads it oftenest will like it best, and he who is acquainted with it, will know the hand wherever he can see it."[12] Might, in other words, the greater challenge we face in prayer be *recognizing* what Wordsworth called "intimations" of the divine, learning the language of God? The poet R. S. Thomas prompted such a consideration, suggesting God may be speaking "in ways we have yet to recognize as speech."[13]

In the sacramental novel *Gilead*, we find a wise old preacher saying this about his grandfather:

> I believe that the old man did indeed have far too narrow an idea of what a vision might be. He may, so to speak, have been too dazzled by the great light of his experience to realize that an impressive sun shines on us all. Perhaps that is the one thing I wish to tell you. Sometimes the visionary aspect of any particular day comes to you in the memory of it, or it opens to you over time. For example, whenever I take a child into my arms to be baptized, I am, so to speak, comprehended in the experience more fully, having seen more of a life, knowing better what it means to affirm the sacredness of the human creature. I believe there are visions that come to us only in memory, in retrospect.[14]

Sometimes the problem may be that our expectations are too paltry, not too grandiose. We so strain to hear the voice in the whirlwind that we fail to see light breaking in the east. We are waiting for the message even as our world has been miraculously reconstituted around us. We are like the character in Walker Percy's novel *The Second Coming*, who is willing to risk his life to find evidence of God's reality. He hears no voice, feels no comfort, and thinks all his prayers have been so many "dead letters sent." Only at the end does he reflect on the improbable love he has found in the most unlikely of places, in a soul as wounded as his own, with whom he finds a solace and communion beyond all expectations. Only then does he think to consider, "Is she a gift and therefore a sign of a giver?"[15] Like Percy's desperate seeker, we too ask but are perhaps not sufficiently open to the myriad ways in which God enacts, rather than articulates, His response.

And sometimes prayer expectations are too grandiose rather than too modest. A friend of ours, caught in the agony of unrelenting depression, discovered that answers can come through surprising, unanticipated avenues. One day, immobilized within the confines of her bedroom, she noticed a dog penned up in a garden opposite. She realized that she had seen him there day after day, confined physically as she was emotionally. She gathered up what courage she had and asked the owners if she could walk their dog. They agreed—and as she strolled the neighborhood day after day, passersby stopped to pet the dog and engage her in conversation. Slowly, imperceptibly, simple human interactions and the laughter of children restored her to the daybreak of mental health. Her despair had opened her heart to forms of revelation she would not have considered earlier.[16]

Another friend recalls years of praying into the void, through adolescence and into his mission. Finally, in spiritual agony, he wrote home, complaining of his own feeling of fraudulence. An unexpected rebuke came back from his mother.

"Enough of this nonsense. This is pure foolishness. Stop this at once. Stop praying with your knees, start praying with your feet." And that was a sweet relief for me. It was complete and total liberation. I took her advice and decided "I'm going to stop doing this thing. I'm going to stop holding a gun to the Lord's head and insisting on a sign. I'm just going to live my life as if the gospel is true." So you must understand: what I did upon reading that letter, was that I made a wager. I decided to bet my entire life that the gospel was true. I decided I would wager my life that the Church is everything it claims it is and live out my life accordingly. So that is what I've done and what I continue to do. . . . The kicker is that in the course of serving and fulfilling priesthood duty, knowledge does in fact come. But for me it has come in ways that were unbidden. Knowledge for me has not arrived because it was beckoned, or because I said "give me a revelation." For me it has come in ways I can barely describe, and never on command, and I'm not even sure that they're sensory or palpable. But I can tell you . . . that I somehow crossed a threshold into an area that I think we can call something more approaching knowledge. When I speak with conviction about our church it's not merely with hope and with faith but with something that is approaching knowledge. That I can tell you. But it's never come on my terms and never come to me on my timetable.[17]

Philip Barlow has written in this regard that "for some of us that test may come in our challenge to keep trying, to keep planting seeds and nurturing them, without feeling any clearly recognizable swelling motions, or spiritual confirmation, but simply enduring in hope and desire until, after long and patient service in love, the joyful taste of the fruit comes 'as a natural sequence to the performance of duty.'"[18]

Finally, perseverance in itself may not be the missing ingredient in prayer. Prayer is more than an attempt to wrest from heaven intellectual clarification or propositional responses to informational questions (though such dialogic revelation has its role in the life of lay seekers and prophets). The prayer that seeks to be the "icepick to break up the frozen sea within us," in Kafka's words,[19] is a miraculous passage across difference. If prayer is to succeed, it must bridge the divide between earth and heaven, a mortal heart and the divine mind. The only way this is possible is for us to relinquish all our preconceptions of how God may choose to answer our entreaties.

Buckling under the agony of Gethsemane, our Lord pled with God to remove the cup before Him. God could not answer Christ's plea for escape from His predicament without compromising the Atonement and the fate of billions. Christ's self-correction, however, in submitting Himself to the Father's judgment ("thy will be done"), did not limit God's ability to succor—it expanded it. The additional words were not a formulaic catchall. They represented genuine submission of mind and heart both to God's cosmic intentions and to the manner of His personal response to a Son in distress. "Answer me how—and in the way—you choose," was His prayer. And it was in response to Christ's openness of that degree and kind that the Father was able to send the angel who ministered to Christ in His agony, "strengthening him."[20] Response—and relief—came to the Savior only when He did not constrain the manner in which the answer came.

CHAPTER 11

TO THE GODLESS AND GUILELESS:

BELIEF AS RISK

•———————•

Go, my beloved children, live your life.
Wounded, faint, bleeding, never yield the strife.
Stunned, fallen—awake, arise, and fight again.
Before you victory stands, with shining train
Of hopes not credible until they are.
Beyond morass and mountains swells the star
Of perfect love—the home of longing heart and brain.

—GEORGE MACDONALD[1]

Oh happy Homer, taking the stars and the Gods for granted.[2]

•———————•

Almost fourteen billion years ago, many scientists maintain, a singularity smaller than an atom spawned a universe of unimaginable vastness. No god brooded over the moment of creation. Neither you nor I nor any form of spirit, intelligence, or mind was present. No consciousness, no life, not the simplest single cell. Hydrogen atoms, single protons bound to single electrons, constituted the most complex form of earliest existence, hurtling through space in their trillions upon trillions.

Several cosmological constants, calibrated with exquisite exactitude, enabled stars to form and then explode, planets to coagulate out of their debris, and teeming seas to incubate life. Life. From twinned electrons and protons fusing with other pairs in the furnace of celestial suns, an earth one day gave birth to you and me with a beating heart, self-awareness, guilt and ecstasy, infinite yearnings and the chilling fear of self-oblivion. Mozart and Shakespeare; the *Requiem Mass* and the poetry of *Romeo and Juliet*. Courage to win the Victoria Cross and brilliance to build rocket ships to the moon. The humor of a young Bill Cosby, the artistry of a Margot Fonteyn,

133

and the stirrings of first love. All from a singularity spewing forth its teeming atoms into the void.

Even nontheist cosmologists concede the astronomically remote odds of myriad cosmological constants appearing in concert to enable the emergence of a life-sustaining universe. Its precision and collective appearance seems to be "astonishingly improbable," a "mysterious collection of pure numbers," "unlikely coincidences" that are nonetheless "essential to the existence of carbon-based" life forms like ourselves, according to the classic treatment of what is called "the anthropic principle."[3] The Astronomer Royal of England says of one such constant in particular, necessary for planets to form, that the attraction of gravity that threatens to collapse the universe is balanced by a countervailing force (Ω) whose "required precision is astonishing." It cannot have differed from its value "by more than one part in a million billion (one in 10^{15})."[4] Richard Dawkins notes that "the origin of life" is "many orders of magnitude more improbable than most people realize";[5] but we are here, nontheists maintain, and so we must be the fortunate fruit of an improbable concatenation of conditions. Perhaps, some argue, given an infinity of universes, one like ours was bound to appear sooner or later. If we were to posit a multiverse of innumerable universes, imagining ours to have the one winning ticket out of trillions of possibilities is only remarkable rather than impossible (though the multiverse is of course itself a nonfalsifiable hypothesis, not a scientific theory). Doubtless, this mind-set holds, given an infinity of time, one of a hundred monkeys would eventually, inadvertently, type the full text of *Hamlet*. We are, in this view, no more than "poor players that strut and fret our hour upon the stage," written into being by the contingencies of plentiful cosmic possibilities.[6] Such, at least, is one possibility.

For the Christian contemporaries of Joseph Smith, a second alternative to such an improbable scenario was a similarly improbable God: a triune Being without body, parts, or passions, One who has existed before the universe itself and is in fact the source of all reality. A God who foreknows all and did, by "His own will, freely, and unchangeably ordain whatsoever comes to pass."[7]

A third alternative is the one proposed by Joseph Smith. A scenario in which an intelligence not absolutely and utterly dissimilar from our own—possibly even the result of cosmic evolution spanning eons of time—presides over our world. As Dawkins allowed himself to speculate, "God indeed can't have just happened, if there are Gods in the universe, they must be the end product of slow incremental processes. If there are beings in the universe that we would treat as Gods, if we met them, . . . they very likely may be so much more advanced than us that we would worship them."[8] Or, as Joseph Smith taught, "We have imagined that God was God from the beginning of all eternity," when in fact, all intelligences progress, "going from a small capacity to a great capacity, from a small degree to another, from grace to grace."[9]

We have at least three propositions, therefore, none of which is self-evidently the only reasonable view of reality. According to the first, in a godless universe, we exist as thinking, feeling, loving human selves, born—without design or larger purpose—of hydrogen atoms hurtling through space that is itself in process of infinite expansion from a primeval singularity smaller than a pinpoint. Natural cosmic and biological processes might have eventuated in our nonexistence, or in our development into utterly different kinds of creatures. We are, in sum, a coincidence.

According to the second, we are creatures of a beginningless God with whom we only metaphorically share image and likeness. For purposes of His own, He created us body and soul at the time of birth, condemned us for an ancient transgression, provides a limited salvation to those fortunate enough to hear and then accept a Savior, and, upon the dissolution of earthly lives and relationships, rewards some with happiness and some with torment.

Or, we find a third option, a Mormon perspective, with five foundational assertions:

First, we find an eternally existing universe presided over by a Deity who embodies the perfect love for which we yearn and toward which we ourselves stretch, the weeping God encountered by Enoch. A Being who literally, and not metaphorically, feels our pain as well as our joy, and is responsive to it. Who made Himself vulnerable, and thus, as the Christian martyr Dietrich Bonhöffer wrote, "wins power and space in the world by his weakness."[10]

Second, we find here a vision of human identity that is rooted in spirit—a refined matter as ancient or as eternal as the rest of our universe. Consciousness itself, our experience of aliveness and introspection and self-awareness and morality and meaning and responsiveness to Beethoven and Schiller's Ode to Joy, suggests a core identity of a radically distinct nature (as philosophers and physicists from Thomas Nagel to Freeman Dyson argue),[11] and one that is eternal in its existence (as the philosopher John McTaggart argued).[12]

Third, a vision of mortality, consistent with the evolving momentum of all nature, that is educative, purposeful, and ennobling. Life as a moral workshop that we enter as willing students, not as unwitting victims of fate or happenstance, not as suffering culprits for an ancient father's and mother's supposed crime. Life as a purposeful sojourn through which we strive toward virtue, acquire wisdom to carry with us, and cultivate relationships to survive the grave.

Fourth, a vision of human potential and worth that is universal. No preordained losers, no predetermined ends, no ceilings of celestial glass. Infinite possibilities that do not depend on the circumstances of mortal birth into a particular place or time or culture. A destiny of eternal growth and increasing joy that God has made—and will continue to make—available to all, even as much as "they are willing to receive." For it is His will that none should be lost.[13]

Finally, a belief that the relationships that are the end of all our human striving—marital love and unity, parental devotion to children stronger than pain or death, friendships of long duration and those recently formed—that all these endure. The conviction that these are too fine, too transcendent to dissipate in the wake of physical dissolution may indeed be wishful, hopeful thinking. But it also seems reasonable, given love's persistent survival amidst the traumas and horrors of history, against the tides of material distractions and the organism's propensity for self-interest, and in light of the otherwise stingy economy of the universe.

These cardinal propositions constitute a holistic paradigm that, remarkably, emerged intact with the advent of Mormonism in 1830—at a moment in religious history when those tenets were not present in any creed in the Christian world. In the absence of spiritual voices in the night, or warm feelings in the bosom, or identifiable revelations of the sort, might these not harmonize with the lived experience and the stubborn claims our heart makes upon us?

Each of the three possibilities provides a map, but only in outline. Each requires—at some point in the process of acceptance and assimilation—that we assemble the scattered pieces of evidence from science, from life experience, from intuition, and from reason into a tentative whole, trusting some sources of meaning and distrusting others. We cannot escape the burden of faith, within or outside the parameters of religious conviction. As another writer has said, "Everyone has to believe something. You don't get to opt out. . . . *That* we will believe is not in question. The question is *what* we will believe in, and why." Of course, he continues, our belief structure may suffer from new evidence, or new challenges. "In that case we do need to adjust our beliefs to accommodate less evidence than we had before. Even in that case, however, we ought not to fool ourselves into thinking that we can simply stop believing. We can only believe in different things."[14]

While spiritual conviction, "testimony," born of heavenly

witness, is one basis for a life of Christian discipleship, it is not the only conceivable basis. If, as Mormon scripture asserts, to some is given to know of Christ's divinity and kindred doctrines, while others are given to believe,[15] then it would appear God is suggesting that the grounds for a reasoned devotion to the gospel are available to those who doubt. These grounds would seem to exist as a convergence of reasonable but not compelling evidence and the innate moral capacity to embrace such evidence. It is a leap not into the dark but into the still murky dawn. If this reading of the scripture is true, then the Lord apparently anticipates—and validates (as have Latter-day Saint apostles in recent remarks)—those who don't feel the full light of spiritual illumination or revelation.[16] And as all have different gifts, it is entirely possible that some who doubt will never in this life acquire the gift of knowledge, of certainty.

Some of us, in other words, are called to live lives of commitment and devotion while dwelling in the realms of belief alone, or harboring the earnest desire to believe. In the perpetual absence of certainty, one may still choose to embrace, and live by, a set of propositions that are aesthetically, morally, and rationally appealing. Even in the absence of certainty, a commitment to the weeping God of Enoch and the gospel of His Son seems a devotion that carries its own intrinsic worth. In fact, we believe its worth is sufficient reason for a life of constant devotion. We understand, and embrace, the opinion of George MacDonald:

> Even if there be no hereafter, I would live my time believing in a grand thing that ought to be true if it is not. And if these be not truths, then is the loftiest part of our nature a waste. Let me hold by the better than the actual, and fall into nothingness off the same precipice with Jesus and Paul and a thousand more, who were lovely in their lives, and with their death make even the nothingness into which they have passed like the garden of the Lord. I will go

further, and say I would rather die forevermore believing as Jesus believed, than live forevermore believing as those that deny Him.[17]

Of course, to believe is to risk error. To trust in a man, or a cause, or a God, is to risk disappointment. To act in faith is to risk failure, betrayal, even humiliation. One great philosopher of the twentieth century, William Clifford, famously insisted that "it is wrong always, everywhere, and for anyone to believe anything upon insufficient evidence."[18] William James responded with words that hinted at a human foible behind the lofty-sounding position:

> He who says "Better to go without belief forever than believe a lie!" merely shows his own preponderant private horror of becoming a dupe. . . . This fear he slavishly obeys. . . . For my own part, I have also a horror of being duped; but I can believe that worse things than being duped may happen to a man in this world. . . . It is like a general informing his soldiers that it is better to keep out of battle forever than to risk a single wound. Not so are victories either over enemies or over nature gained. Our errors are surely not such awfully solemn things. In a world where we are so certain to incur them in spite of all our caution, a certain lightness of heart seems healthier than this excessive nervousness on their behalf.[19]

"Cheerful insecurity" was the name C. S. Lewis gave to this attitude of the Christian disciple.[20]

The question is, do we love what is true, what is good, what is beautiful, more than we fear the possible error our embrace of those things risks? No human relationship can carry any guarantees of success, but the vulnerability to which we expose ourselves in love is to a large degree the measure of that love. So it is also with the gesture of faith. Faith, wrote Milton Steinberg, "is the axis about which we move—an axis that must be posited as an act of will. The fate of man determines whether he has located it properly."[21] This is the sense in which, as Thomas Carlyle pointed out, we are all religious.[22] We all exhibit our faith commitments by the way we live, and those commitments are oriented around a value or set of values, a belief or set of beliefs, by which we guide our lives. We may posit reason as the highest good. Or pleasure. Or love or kindness. But no foundation is without an act of faith to sustain it. The five propositions summarized above constitute the most reasonable axis we have found around which to orient our lives. They are the seeds, we believe, that have borne fruit that is good—what Alma calls a "real," "discernible" good.[23]

The question may remain, how does one lock onto the propositional assertions of a restored gospel that is also laden with claims about gold plates and the Book of Abraham and a male priesthood and a polygamous past and a thousand other details we may find difficult? Perhaps, with those five core ideas in mind, one might focus on the message rather than the messenger. One might consider that the contingencies of history and culture and the human element will always constitute the garment in which God's word and will are clothed. And one might refuse to allow our desire for the perfect to be the enemy of the present good. Finally, we might ask ourselves, with the early disciples, "to whom [else] shall we go?"

The worst risk such a life of faith entails is not that such a life might be wrong—but that it might be incomprehensible to those unprepared to take such a risk. As Cardinal Emmanuel Suhard wrote, "To be a witness does not consist in engaging in propaganda, nor even in stirring people up, but in being a living mystery. It means to live in such a way that one's life would not make sense if God did not exist."[24]

DOUBT AND DISCIPLESHIP

·———·

For man to act as if his soul did see
The very brightness of eternity;
For man to act as if his love did burn
Above the spheres, even while it's in its urn;
For man to act even in the wilderness
As if he did those sovereign joys possess
Which do at once confirm, stir up, inflame
And perfect angels—having not the same!
It doth increase the value of his deeds;
In this a man a Seraphim exceeds.
To act on obligations yet unknown,
To act upon rewards as yet unshown,
To keep commands whose beauty's yet unseen,
To cherish and retain a zeal between
Sleeping and waking, shows a constant care;
And that a deeper love, a love so rare
That no eye-service may with it compare.
The angels, who are faithful while they view
His glory, know not what themselves would do,

Were they in our estate! A dimmer light
Perhaps would make them err as well as we;
And in the coldness of a darker night
Forgetful and lukewarm themselves might be.
Our very rust shall cover us with gold,
Our dust shall sparkle while their eyes behold
The glory springing from a feeble state,
Where mere belief doth, if not conquer fate,
Surmount, and pass what it doth antedate.

—THOMAS TRAHERNE[1]

I think there is no suffering greater than what is caused by the doubts of those who want to believe.[2]

N ot once, but twice, the Lord prefaced His commandment that we strengthen each other with this explanation: "As all have not faith."[3] He thus acknowledged that even among His modern disciples, there would be—and must be—room for those who live in doubt. If our faith is damaged beyond repair or lacking altogether, if we cannot find it in ourselves to proclaim the gospel or embrace its tenets, we can still live its essence. Many in the Church and world are doing just that. Just as some have entertained "angels unawares," so might we well be exercising faith unbeknown. Faith is lived, not thought.

The Spaniard Miguel de Unamuno wrote his most poignant story about a humble priest who forsakes advancement and acclaim, a career brimming with promise and potential, to minister to the needs of an impoverished rural flock. All the while, he harbors a dreadful secret in his heart. For the saintly Don Manuel has lived his whole priestly life devoid of faith in God, as he confides in anguish to his closest friend and confidante, Angelina. Her brother, she later learns, the priest's assistant in a lifelong ministry, lived and died in the same valley of faithless despair. As she sets out to write the story of "Saint Manuel, the Good, Martyr," and his unheralded associate, she meditates on her firsthand "experience with saintliness." She realizes that, although they "died believing they did not believe," that in fact "they actually believed, in active . . . desolation." The keyword is "active." They lived out their faith, even if they didn't *feel* it. And who can doubt the more important of the two? "I do not know," the memorialist concluded, "what . . . caused them to believe they were unbelievers."[4] Only when the final story of a doubter's life and ministry is told, only then might she be in a position to say what she believed, as her faith is finally revealed in the lives of those she touched.

We all have known our share of broken hearts and silent skies. We pass through our deserts, and we often labor to recall the sweet waters we have tasted along the way. Perhaps, when our faith or our desire to believe is at its lowest ebb, we might consider the meaning of those words, "blessed is he that believeth . . . without being brought to know . . . or even compelled to know, before they will believe."[5] Perhaps these words are telling us there is a type of flower that can bloom only in the desert of doubt. Faith that we elect to profess in the absence of certainty is an offering that is entirely free, unconditioned, and utterly authentic. Such a gesture represents our considered and chosen response to the universe, our assent to what we find beautiful and worthy and deserving of our risk.

We have learned to relish a commitment that is born of faith freely chosen rather than of certainty compelled by evidence. As we have written elsewhere, we believe deeply in the value of faith as a choice. That the call to faith is a summons to engage the heart, to attune it to resonate in sympathy with principles and values and ideals that we devoutly hope are true, and that we have reasonable but not certain grounds for believing to be true. And that what we choose to embrace, to be responsive to, is the purest reflection of what we love. We are prepared, with these things in mind, to risk "paying the universe a compliment it doesn't deserve."[6]

So here, in sum, are the principal reasons for "the hope that is in us." We agree with Nathaniel Hawthorne, who believed that "our Creator would never have made such lovely days and have given us the deep hearts to enjoy them, above and beyond all thought, unless we were meant to be immortal."[7] And if we are immortal, no eternal existence makes sense separate and apart from an eternal community of loved ones, presided over by heavenly parents who set their hearts upon us. We could never love a God "without body, parts, or passions," who does not Himself feel love, or grief, or joy, or gladness. Christianity gave us a God who was willing to die on behalf of His creation; Joseph Smith added to that conception a God who intends our full participation in "the divine nature," who will bestow upon every single one of His children all that they "are willing to receive," and who made Himself vulnerable enough to weep at our pain and misery. That is a God to whom we are powerfully drawn, and whom we gladly worship.

We have seen the power of the gospel to transform human life. We can affirm, as Gerard Manley Hopkins did, that "Christ plays in ten thousand places, lovely in limbs and lovely in eyes, not his, to the Father, through the features of men's faces."[8] In new converts and returned missionaries, who in their testimonies unexpectedly speak "with the tongues of angels," a simple eloquence not of their own resources. In the parting words of a beloved friend near death, before whom the veil grows suddenly thin to transparency. In lives transformed and redirected, then imbued with sudden beauty, to rival anything narrated by an Elizabeth Gaskell or a Victor Hugo.

Joseph Smith said, "You say honey is sweet, and so do I. I can also taste the spirit of eternal life. I know it is good; and when I tell you of these things which were given me by inspiration of the Holy Spirit, you are bound to receive them as sweet, and rejoice more and more."[9] We believe the doctrine of the Restoration to be true for the same reason: It tastes good.

NOTES

EPIGRAPH

Fyodor Dostoevsky, *The Unpublished Dostoevsky: Diaries and Notebooks* (Ann Arbor: Ardis, 1976), 175.

INTRODUCTION
PARADIGMS AND PREMISES: STARTING OFF ON THE WRONG FOOT

1. Julian of Norwich, *Showings*, ed. Denise N. Baker (New York: Norton, 2005), XIII.40, p. 55. We modernize some spellings and occasionally syntax.
2. Julian, *Showings*, XIII.27, p. 39.
3. Julian, *Showings*, XVI.78, p. 117.
4. Moses 6:55.
5. Genesis 3:22.
6. W. E. Riter to James E. Talmage, 22 August 1921. In B. H. Roberts, *Studies of the Book of Mormon*, 2nd ed., ed. Brigham D. Madsen (Salt Lake City: Signature, 1992), 35.
7. B. H. Roberts to Heber J. Grant et al., 29 December 1921. In Roberts, *Studies of the Book of Mormon*, 46.
8. Jacob 7:4.
9. For the number and discussion of geographical references, see John Sorenson, "The Book of Mormon as a Mesoamerican Record," in Noel B. Reynolds, ed., *Book of Mormon Authorship Revisited: The Evidence for Ancient Origins* (Provo, UT: Foundation for Ancient Research and Mormon Studies [FARMS], 1997), 392.
10. Daniel C. Dennett, *Intuition Pumps and Other Tools for Thinking* (New York: Norton, 2013), 20.

11. D&C 8:11; 8:1.
12. Andrew F. Ehat and Lyndon W. Cook, eds., *The Words of Joseph Smith: The Contemporary Accounts of the Nauvoo Discourses of the Prophet Joseph Smith* (Orem, Utah: Grandin, 1994), 319.
13. 2 Timothy 3:7.
14. Hans Georg Gadamer, *Truth and Method* (London: Continuum, 2004), 299.

CHAPTER 1
OF METHOD AND MAPS: THE USE AND ABUSE OF REASON

1. George Santayana, "O World, Thou Choosest," in *Sonnets and Other Verses* (New York: Duffield, 1906), 5.
2. Virginia Woolf, *To the Lighthouse* (New York: Harcourt, Brace & World, 1927), 32.
3. "Because of *Antigone*, tradition relates, the people of Athens elected [Sophocles] the next year to high office." Sophocles, *Antigone*, trans. Richard Emil Braun (New York: Oxford University Press, 1973), 3.
4. Those descriptions are from William Hazlitt, "On the Feeling of Immortality in Youth," *Literary Remains* (London: Saunders and Otley, 1836), 2:268; Victor Shklovsky, "Art as Technique," *Russian Formalist Criticism* (Lincoln: University of Nebraska, 1965), 12; Percy B. Shelley, "The Defense of Poetry," *Essays, Letters from Abroad* (Philadelphia: Lea and Blanchard, 1840), 1:59.
5. William Wordsworth, "Ode: Intimations of Immortality," in *Poetical Works* (Oxford: Oxford University Press, 1989), 499.
6. Charles Darwin, *The Descent of Man* (New York: Appleton, 1871), 162.
7. George Gordon, Lord Byron, *Cain* III.i, in *Complete Poetical Works* (Boston: Houghton Mifflin, 1905), 648.
8. William A. Luijpen, *Phenomenology and Humanism* (Pittsburgh: Duquesne University Press, 1966), 65.
9. Charles Taylor, "Gadamer and the Human Sciences," in Robert J. Dostal, ed., *The Cambridge Companion to Gadamer* (Cambridge: Cambridge University Press, 2002), 128, 132.
10. Julian of Norwich, *Showings*, ed. Denise N. Baker (New York: Norton, 2005), XIV.41, p. 57.
11. Philip Barlow, "Ten Commandments for Balancing the Life of the Mind and Spirit on Campus," in *A Twenty-Something's Guide to Spirituality*, comp. Jacob Werrett and David Read (Salt Lake City: Deseret Book, 2007), 154–55.
12. Luijpen, *Phenomenology*, 6–7.
13. Phillip F. Schewe, *Maverick Genius: The Pioneering Odyssey of Freeman Dyson* (New York: St. Martin's, 2013), 250.
14. The study by Elaine Howard Ecklund, a sociologist at Rice University, involved more than nine thousand respondents and was first reported in February 2014. "Faith and Reason," *The Economist* (22 February 2014), 28.
15. David Hume, *Inquiry Concerning the Principles of Morals* (La Salle, Illinois:

Open Court, 1960 [1777]), part I. Cited in Jonathan Haidt, *The Righteous Mind: Why Good People Are Divided by Politics and Religion* (New York: Pantheon, 2012), 48. Haidt's is a brilliant exposition of the basis of human beliefs in moral intuition rather than reason.

16. David Hume, *A Treatise of Human Nature* (London: Penguin, 1969 [1739–40]), 462. Cited in Haidt, *Righteous Mind,* 25.

17. Martin Rees, *Just Six Numbers: The Deep Forces That Shape the Universe* (New York: Basic Books, 2000), 92–93.

CHAPTER 2

ON PROVOCATION AND PEACE:
OF LIFE'S FUNDAMENTAL INCOMPLETENESS

1. Emily Dickinson, "The Bible Is an Antique Volume," in *Complete Poems* (Boston: Little, Brown, 1960), 185.

2. José Ortega y Gasset, *What Is Philosophy?* trans. Mildred Adams (New York: Norton, 1960), 252.

3. William Blake, "The Lamb," in *The Complete Poems* (London: Longman, 1989), 65.

4. William Blake, "The Tiger," in *Complete Poems,* 214–15.

5. Christopher Marlowe, *Dr. Faustus,* I.i (New York: Signet, 1969), 27.

6. Matthew 5; 11:8; 20:22; 10:35; 2 Peter 1:13; 3:1. Biblical citations are from the King James Version unless otherwise indicated.

7. Jeffrey R. Holland, "The Cost—and Blessings—of Discipleship," *Ensign,* May 2014, 7.

8. See Matthew 8:21–22; 10:34.

9. John 6:60, 66–67.

10. The quotation is from the narrative of John Chislett, in. B. H. Roberts, *Comprehensive History of the Church of Jesus Christ of Latter-day Saints,* 6 vols. (Provo, Utah: Brigham Young University Press, 1965), 4:89.

11. Andrew F. Ehat and Lyndon W. Cook, eds., *The Words of Joseph Smith: The Contemporary Accounts of the Nauvoo Discourses of the Prophet Joseph Smith* (Orem, Utah: Grandin, 1994), 183.

12. John Ciardi, "The Gift," in *Collected Poems,* ed. Edward M. Cifelli (Fayetteville, Arkansas: University of Arkansas Press, 1997), 225.

13. Flannery O'Connor, "To Louise Abbot," in *The Habit of Being: Letters of Flannery O'Connor,* ed. Sally Fitzgerald (New York: Farrar, Straus, Giroux, 1988), 354.

14. Matthew 16:24.

15. Holland, "The Cost," 7.

16. See 2 Nephi 2:14.

17. William James, "The Will to Believe," in *The Will to Believe and Other Essays* (New York: Longmans, 1919), 11.

18. Michael Novak, *No One Sees God* (New York: Doubleday, 2008), 65.

19. 1 John 3:2.

20. Brigham Young, *Complete Discourses*, ed. Richard S. Van Wagoner (Salt Lake City: Smith-Pettit Foundation, 2009), 2:890.

21. Dennis Rasmussen, *The Lord's Question: Thoughts on the Life of Response* (n.p.: Keter Foundation, 2001), 11.

22. Young, *Complete Discourses*, 2:1009.

23. William Wordsworth, "Ode: Intimations of Immortality," in *Poetical Works* (Oxford: Oxford University Press, 1989), 460.

24. Isabella Fenwick, in Jared Curtis, ed., *The Fenwick Notes of William Wordsworth* (London: Bristol Classical Press, 1993), 61–62.

25. William Wordsworth, "It Is Beauteous Evening," in *Poetical Works*, 205.

26. Wordsworth, "Ode," in *Poetical Works*, 461.

27. Ehat and Cook, eds., *Words*, 345.

28. Richard P. Feynman, *QED: The Strange Theory of Light and Matter* (Princeton: Princeton University Press, 1988), 10.

29. John 6:68.

30. 1 Nephi 11:17.

CHAPTER 3

OF SADDUCEES AND SACRAMENTS:
THE ROLE AND FUNCTION OF THE CHURCH

1. William Wordsworth, "Nuns Fret Not," in *Poetical Works* (Oxford: Oxford University Press, 1989), 199.

2. William H. Willimon and Stanley Hauerwas, *Preaching to Strangers* (Louisville: Westminster/John Knox Press, 1992), 75.

3. "The Hospitaler" (David Thewlis), in *Kingdom of Heaven*, dir. Ridley Scott, 2005.

4. Thomas Carlyle, *On Heroes and Hero Worship* (London: Chapman and Hall, 1840), 4–5.

5. James 1:27.

6. A useful metaphor, stolen from one of Nathaniel Givens's blog posts.

7. Acts 15:1, 10.

8. Luke 22:19.

9. Genesis 22:5.

10. Matthew 2:11.

11. 2 Samuel 24:24.

12. Dietrich Bonhoeffer, "Costly Grace," in *The Cost of Discipleship* (New York: Simon and Schuster, 1995), 43–44.

13. George Herbert, "The Pulley," in *The Poems of George Herbert*, ed. F. E. Hutchinson (London: Oxford University Press, 1979), 150.

14. Alma 22:18.

15. The plaque was translated from the Latin by "Mr T. Young." The translation is presently on display in the York Minster.

16. Job 34:14; 2 Nephi 26:24; see also Moses 7:28; 1:39.
17. See his "Divine Authority and the Conditions of Salvation," http://publications
    .maxwellinstitute.byu.edu/fullscreen/?pub=2324&index=1&keyword
    =summer%20seminar%20working%20papers%202013.
18. Isaiah 33:14.
19. C. S. Lewis, *Perelandra* (New York: Scribner, 1972), 101.
20. Robert B. Thompson, 5 Oct. 1840, in Andrew F. Ehat and Lyndon W. Cook,
    eds., *The Words of Joseph Smith: The Contemporary Accounts of the Nauvoo
    Discourses of the Prophet Joseph Smith* (Orem, Utah: Grandin, 1994), 39.
21. *Times and Seasons* 4 (15 September 1843): 331.
22. Willard Richards, Joseph Smith Diary, 9 October 1843, in Ehat and Cook,
    eds., *Words*, 254.
23. "Sadducees," *Encyclopaedia Judaica* (Jerusalem: Keter, 1972), 14:621. The anal-
    ogy with Mormons is hardly fully apt. Sadducees rejected the Resurrection,
    angels, and the supernatural in general.

CHAPTER 4
OF CANONS AND CANNONS: THE USE AND ABUSE OF SCRIPTURE

1. Emily Dickinson, "The Bible Is an Antique Volume," in *Complete Poems*
   (Boston: Little, Brown, 1960), 644.
2. *Oxford English Dictionary*, s.v. "cannon," "canon."
3. 2 Timothy 3:16.
4. See Psalm 119:105.
5. Deuteronomy 25:5.
6. Leviticus 18:16.
7. *Martin Luther: Selections from His Writings* (New York: Random House, 2011),
   18.
8. Romans 1:17.
9. James 2:20.
10. D&C 121:16, 21.
11. John 2:15.
12. See also 1 Chronicles 21:15; Jonah 3:10, NRSV; Matthew 27:5; Acts 1:18;
    2 Kings 24:8; 2 Chronicles 36:9; Proverbs 26:5; 26:4; emphasis added.
13. 1 Nephi 19:6.
14. 1 Nephi 13:28.
15. D&C 91:1.
16. Andrew F. Ehat and Lyndon W. Cook, eds., *The Words of Joseph Smith: The
    Contemporary Accounts of the Nauvoo Discourses of the Prophet Joseph Smith*
    (Orem, Utah: Grandin, 1994), 345.
17. Ehat and Cook, eds., *Words*, 211.
18. *Lectures on Faith* (Salt Lake City: Deseret Book, 1985), 38.
19. Richard Elliott Friedman, *Who Wrote the Bible?* (New York: Harper & Row,
    1989), 59–60.

20. Abraham J. Heschel, *The Prophets* (New York: Harper and Row, 1962), 57. Heschel is here citing Exodus 3:7.
21. "The Fountain of Knowledge," in *An appeal to the inhabitants of the state of New York* (Nauvoo, Illinois: John Taylor, 1844), 17.
22. George MacDonald, "The Higher Faith," in *Unspoken Sermons* (Whitehorn, California: Johannesen, 2004), 37.
23. D&C 68:3.
24. Joseph Smith, 25 March 1839, in Manuscript History of the Church (Church History Library), C-1, 907.

CHAPTER 5
ON PROPHECY AND PROPHETS: THE PERILS OF HERO WORSHIP

1. George Herbert, "The Priesthood," in *The Poems of George Herbert*, ed. F. E. Hutchinson (London: Oxford University Press, 1979), 151.
2. Fyodor Dostoevsky, *The Brothers Karamazov* (New York: Penguin, 1978), 1:297–98.
3. Thomas Carlyle, *On Heroes and Hero Worship* (London: Chapman and Hall, 1840), 216, 15, 291.
4. Carlyle, *Heroes*, 3.
5. Carlyle, *Heroes*, 16.
6. Dostoevsky, *Brothers Karamazov*, 2:31.
7. Matthew 19:21.
8. Dostoevsky, *Brothers Karamazov*, 1:271.
9. Brigham Young, *Complete Discourses*, ed. Richard S. Van Wagoner (Salt Lake City: Smith-Pettit Foundation, 2009), 2:1008.
10. Young, *Complete Discourses*, 4:1941.
11. J. Golden Kimball, in Conference Report, April 1904, 97.
12. The offensive statement was published in *The Improvement Era*, June 1945. Smith responded in a letter to J. Raymond Cope, a Unitarian leader who expressed concern. *Dialogue* 19.1 (Spring 1986): 35–39.
13. D. Todd Christofferson, "The Doctrine of Christ," *Ensign*, May 2012, 88.
14. The remark was in President Uchtdorf's address in general conference, 5 October 2013. The two articles were Laurie Goodstein, "A Top Mormon Leader Acknowledges the Church 'Made Mistakes,'" *New York Times*, 5 October 2013; Laurie Goodstein, "A Leader's Admission of 'Mistakes' Heartens Some Doubting Mormons," *New York Times*, 8 October 2013. Goodstein reported being "deluged" with letters from Mormons angry at her reportage of that statement. Personal interview, 8 October 2013.
15. See Exodus 2:12. Some of these episodes involve divine complicity, according to the Bible. Other examples, like Rachel's theft of her father's idols (Genesis 31) and Jacob's trickery to amass wealth (Genesis 30), do not.
16. See Numbers 20:7–13.
17. See Jonah 4.

18. Galatians 2:11–14, NRSV.

19. Acts 15:37–39.

20. Manuscript History of the Church (Church History Library), D-1, pp. 1555–57.

21. *Joseph Smith Papers: Histories*, Volume 1, eds. Dean C. Jessee, Ronald K. Esplin, and Richard L. Bushman (Salt Lake City: Church Historian's Press, 2012), 220.

22. D&C 3:6.

23. D&C 3:6–7; 24:2.

24. In Neal A. Maxwell, "Out of Obscurity," *Ensign*, November 1984, 10; Brigham Young, in *Journal of Discourses*, 26 vols. (Liverpool, England: Franklin D. Richards and Samuel W. Richards, 1851–86; repr. Salt Lake City, 1974), 4:297.

25. In Maxwell, "Out of Obscurity," 10.

26. 2 Peter 1:4.

27. Parley P. Pratt, *Mormonism Unveiled* (New York: Pratt, 1838), 27.

28. 2 Nephi 4:34; emphasis added.

29. Neal A. Maxwell, "Jesus, the Perfect Mentor," *Ensign*, February 2001, 13.

30. Edward Beecher, *The Conflict of Ages* (New York: Phillips, Sampson and Co., 1853), 552.

31. Judges 8:22, 23; emphasis added.

32. Judges 8:27.

33. D&C 124:1; emphasis added.

34. Wilford Woodruff, *Collected Discourses*, ed. Brian H. Stuy (n.p.: B. H. S. Publishing, 1999), 4:72.

35. Abraham J. Heschel, *The Prophets* (New York: HarperCollins, 2001), 31. Cited in Philip Barlow, "The Mind and the Spirit," in *Oxford Handbook to Mormonism*, eds. Terryl Givens and Philip Barlow (New York: Oxford University Press, forthcoming).

36. The manuscript version of section 93 is typical: it is written in the hand of Orson Hyde, with emendations by Oliver Cowdery, Orson Hyde, William W. Phelps, Frederick G. Williams, an unidentified fifth editor, and Joseph Smith. See *Joseph Smith Papers: Revelations and Translations; Manuscript Revelation Books*, eds. Robin Scott Jensen, Robert J. Woodward, and Steven C. Harper (Salt Lake City: Church Historian's Press, 2009), 524–31.

37. To William W. Phelps, 27 November 1832, in Dean C. Jessee, ed., *Personal Writings of Joseph Smith* (Salt Lake City: Deseret Book, 2002), 287.

38. Andrew F. Ehat and Lyndon W. Cook, eds., *The Words of Joseph Smith: The Contemporary Accounts of the Nauvoo Discourses of the Prophet Joseph Smith* (Orem, Utah: Grandin, 1994), 5.

39. Jessee W. Crosby, in Hyrum L. Andrus and Helen Mae Andrus, *They Knew the Prophet: Personal Accounts from over 100 People Who Knew Joseph Smith* (Salt Lake City: Bookcraft, 1974), 140.

NOTES

40. The story was related by J. Reuben Clark Jr., "When Are Church Leaders' Words Entitled to Claim of Scripture," *Church News*, 31 July 1954, 9–10, and repeated by Christofferson, "Doctrine of Christ," 88–89.
41. *The Instructor*, June 1945, 259, written on 17 January 1878. Cited in David John Buerger, "The Adam-God Doctrine," *Dialogue: A Journal of Mormon Thought* 15.1 (Spring 1982): 34–35.
42. D&C 43:12.
43. D&C 18:8–9.
44. D&C 21:6.

CHAPTER 6
ON DELEGATION AND DISCIPLESHIP: THE RING OF PHARAOH

1. George Herbert, "The Priesthood," in *The Poems of George Herbert*, ed. F. E. Hutchinson (London: Oxford University Press, 1979), 151.
2. Exodus 3:11–12.
3. Genesis 41:42.
4. Genesis 41:44, NRSV.
5. Austin Farrer, "Infallibility and Historical Tradition," in *The Truth-Seeking Heart*, ed. Ann Loades and Robert MacSwain (Norwich: Canterbury Press, 2006), 83.
6. From Henry J. Eyring, *Mormon Scientist: The Life and Faith of Henry Eyring* (Salt Lake City: Deseret Book, 2007), 4.
7. Farrer, "Infallibility," 83–84.
8. D&C 21:5; emphasis added.
9. Andrew F. Ehat and Lyndon W. Cook, eds., *The Words of Joseph Smith: The Contemporary Accounts of the Nauvoo Discourses of the Prophet Joseph Smith* (Orem, Utah: Grandin, 1994), 132.
10. Personal conversation reported to authors by Robert L. Millet.
11. D&C 24:1, 7, 8.
12. Farrer, "Infallibility," 84.
13. Farrer, "Infallibility," 84.
14. B. H. Roberts, "Relation of Inspiration and Revelation to Church Government," *Improvement Era*, March 1905, 365–66.
15. Nathaniel Givens, "Epistemology and Stuff: Everyday Mormon Theology," MS.
16. D. Todd Christofferson, "The Doctrine of Christ," *Ensign*, May 2012, 89, citing "When Are Church Leaders' Words Entitled to Claim of Scripture," *Church News*, 31 July 1954, 9–10; D&C 21:5.
17. These words he wrote in the margins of a prayer book while awaiting execution in the Tower. Thomas More, *Sadness of Christ* (New York: Scepter, 1993), xvii.
18. Farrer, "Infallibility," 84.
19. D&C 122:9.

20. 2 Nephi 2:2.
21. CES Fireside (1 May 2005), Oakland, California.
22. Letter of Vilate Kimball, 30 June 1844, in Ronald K. Esplin, "Life in Nauvoo, June 1844: Vilate Kimball's Martyrdom Letters," *BYU Studies* 19.2 (1979): 238.
23. Jeffrey R. Holland, "Lord, I Believe," *Ensign*, May 2013, 94.
24. Dieter F. Uchtdorf, "Come, Join with Us," *Ensign*, November 2013, 22.

CHAPTER 7
MORMONS AND MONOPOLIES:
HOLY PERSONS "YE KNOW NOT OF"

1. Emily Dickinson, "Read, Sweet, How Others Strove," in *Complete Poems* (Boston: Little, Brown, 1960), 119–20.
2. Andrew F. Ehat and Lyndon W. Cook, eds., *The Words of Joseph Smith: The Contemporary Accounts of the Nauvoo Discourses of the Prophet Joseph Smith* (Orem, Utah: Grandin, 1994), 381–82. Smith was certainly correct, from a Mormon perspective. Contrary to a popular Mormon narrative that sees the Reformation as paving the way for the Restoration, Luther, Calvin, and others in fact shaped Reformation theology in a direction much further removed from the teachings Smith would propound than Catholicism ever was. They did this by emphasizing a God "without body, parts, or passions," human depravity, the Bible as the only source of authority, and salvation by faith alone.
3. Stendahl's "Three Rules of Religious Understanding" were (1) ask adherents, not enemies, for information; (2) don't compare your best to their worst; and (3) leave room for "holy envy." They are unsourced but widely disseminated and attributed to remarks he made at a 1985 press conference in Stockholm where he was serving as a Lutheran bishop.
4. See Matthew 12:39; 23:27; 15:7; 23:33; John 8:44.
5. These examples and worse are cited in Robert Michael, *Holy Hatred* (New York: Palgrave, 2006).
6. John Knox, "The Order and Doctrine of the General Fast," in David Laing, ed., *The Works of John Knox* (Edinburgh: J. Thin, 1895), 6:404.
7. John Calvin, *Steward of God's Covenant: Selected Writings*, ed. John F. Thornton (New York: Random House, 2006), 266.
8. Joseph Ivimey, *A History of the English Baptists* (London: Ivimey, 1811), 1:169.
9. Robert Mansel, *Free Thoughts upon Methodists, Actors, and the Influence of the Stage* (Hull: Mansel and Craggs, 1814), 5–6.
10. *The Enthusiasm of Methodists and Papists Considered by Bishop Lavington*, ed. R. Polwhele (London: A. J. Valpy, 1820), 225–28.
11. Izaak Walton, *The works of that learned and judicious divine, Mr. Richard Hooker* (Oxford: Oxford University Press, 1836), 2:476.
12. Philip Schaff, *The Creeds of Christendom: The Evangelical Protestant Creeds* (New York: Harper & Brothers, 1877), 487.

NOTES

13. Cited in Grant Underwood, *The Millenarian World of Early Mormonism* (Champaign: University of Illinois Press, 1999), 54.

14. Edward Beecher, *Concord of Ages: or The Individual and Organic Harmony of God and Man* (New York: Derby and Jackson, 1860), 92.

15. Richard Sherlock, "A Mormon Scholar's Journey to Catholic Faith," "On the Square," *First Things*, 30 August 2012, http://www.firstthings.com /onthesquare/2012/08/a-mormon-scholarrsquos-journey-to-catholic-faith. He quoted the kindred complaint of Edwin Firmage.

16. D&C 49:8; emphasis added.

17. D&C 10:53–55.

18. Book of Commandments 4:5. Received March 1829.

19. Revelation 12:6, 14; emphasis added.

20. D&C 5:14.

21. Matthew 13:52.

22. Julian of Norwich, *Showings*, ed. Denise N. Baker (New York: Norton, 2005), XIV.51, p. 71.

23. Thomas Traherne, "Innocence," in *Selected Writings of Thomas Traherne*, ed. Dick Davis (Manchester: Fyfield, 1980), 24–26.

24. *Millennial Star* 3.11 (March 1843): 177.

25. John Taylor, in *Journal of Discourses*, 26 vols. (Liverpool, England: Franklin D. Richards and Samuel W. Richards, 1851–86; repr. Salt Lake City, 1974), 16:197–98.

26. Brigham Young, *Complete Discourses*, ed. Richard S. Van Wagoner (Salt Lake City: Smith-Pettit Foundation, 2009), 3:1480.

27. "The Religion of the Ancients," *Times and Seasons* 4.9 (15 March 1843): 136; Not the Prophet, S.T.P., "To the Editor," *Times and Seasons* 5.8 (15 April 1844): 503.

28. Ehat and Cook, eds., *Words*, 360.

29. D&C 76:38–39.

30. Young, *Complete Discourses*, 1:569.

31. Wilford Woodruff, *Collected Discourses*, ed. Brian H. Stuy (n.p.: B. H. S. Publishing, 1999), 4:74.

32. Abraham H. Cannon journal, 5 April 1894. Cited in Stuy, ed., *Collected Discourses*, 4:68.

33. Lorenzo Snow, in Conference Report, April 1901, 3.

34. *Church News*, 23 April 1960, 3.

35. Henry B. Eyring, "To My Grandchildren," *Ensign*, November 2013, 71; quoting George Q. Cannon, *Contributor*, October 1890, 476.

36. Young, *Complete Discourses*, 5:2960. Warren Foote recorded that one "Landon and others had been cut off for rejecting the vision concerning the three glories." *Autobiography* (Mesa: Dale Foote, 1997), 5.

37. Matthew 20:12.

38. Boyd K. Packer, "The Brilliant Morning of Forgiveness," *Ensign*, November 1995.

39. D&C 138:58.

40. Remarks attributed to Krister Stendahl by Daniel Peterson, http://www.fairlds .org/authors/johnson-cooper/breaking-the-rules-of-the-lds-faith. Stendahl in fact wrote the article "Baptism for the Dead" for *Encyclopedia of Mormonism*, 4 vols. (New York: Macmillan, 1992), 1:97.

41. G. K. Chesterton, *Orthodoxy* (New York: Dover, 2004), 12.

CHAPTER 8
SPIRITUALITY AND SELF-SUFFICIENCY:
FIND YOUR WATERING PLACE

1. Robert Frost, "Directive," in *Poetry*, ed. Edward Connery Lathem (New York: Holt, Rinehart, and Winston, 1969), 377–79.

2. Proverbs 5:15.

3. Sterling McMurrin, *The Theological Foundations of the Mormon Religion* (Salt Lake City: University of Utah Press, 1965), 52.

4. Cited in Philip Yancey, *Prayer* (Grand Rapids: Zondervan, 2006), 24.

5. Boyd K. Packer, "Let Them Govern Themselves," address given 30 March 1990, http://oneclimbs.com/2013/07/03/let-them-govern-themselves-by -boyd-k-packer/; he repeated the theme in a later address: "Perhaps we have been over-programming stable families to meet the needs of those with problems. We must seek a better way" ("Teach Them Correct Principles," *Ensign*, May 1990, 90).

6. Joseph Milner, *The History of the Church of Christ*, vol.1 (London: R. B. Seeley and W. Burnside, 1834), v; vol. 2 (Boston: Farrand, Mallory, and Co., 1809), v.

7. Samuel Taylor Coleridge, quoted in Richard Holmes, *Coleridge: Darker Reflections* (New York: Pantheon, 1998), 399.

8. John Calvin, *Institutes* 4.1.7, trans. Henry Beveridge (Peabody, Massachusetts: Hendrickson, 2008), 677.

9. Letter 46, in Robin Waterfield, ed., *Jacob Boehme* (Berkeley: North Atlantic Books, 2001), 16.

10. D&C 76:67.

11. D&C 27:5–14.

12. D&C 10:53–55.

13. D&C 88:118; 2 Nephi 29:10.

14. George MacDonald, "The Higher Faith," in *Unspoken Sermons* (Whitehorn, California: Johannesen, 2004), 35–36.

15. MacDonald, "Higher Faith," 43.

16. MacDonald, "Higher Faith," 37.

17. Kenneth W. Godfrey, "A Note on the Nauvoo Library and Literary Institute," *BYU Studies* 14 (Spring 1974): 386–89.

18. Douglas L. Callister, "Our Refined Heavenly Home," *Ensign*, June 2009, 56.

NOTES

19. Spencer W. Kimball, "When I Look Back: To Camilla," in Edward L. Kimball, "Spencer W. Kimball and Poetry," *BYU Studies* 25.4 (1985): 162.
20. Brigham Young, in *Journal of Discourses*, 26 vols. (Liverpool, England: Franklin D. Richards and Samuel W. Richards, 1851–86; repr. Salt Lake City, 1974), 7:271.
21. Gregory Nazianzen, "Oration 37," trans. Charles Gordon Browne and James Edward Swallow, in Philip Schaff, ed., *Nicene and Post-Nicene Fathers of the Christian Church*, second series (Peabody, MA: Hendrickson, 1999), 7:338.
22. Anonymous, private correspondence, 10 April 2014.
23. Theodore Roosevelt, as quoted in Thomas Herbert Russell, *Life and Work of Theodore Roosevelt* (n.p.: L. H. Walter, 1919), 257.
24. D&C 29:32.
25. Leonard J. Arrington and Davis Bitton, *Saints without Halos* (Salt Lake City: Signature, 1981), 61.
26. Anne Lamott, *Traveling Mercies: Some Thoughts on Faith* (New York: Anchor Books, 2001), 134. Lamott's expression referred to the decision to not forgive.
27. 2 Nephi 4:27.
28. Brigham Young, *Complete Discourses*, ed. Richard S. Van Wagoner (Salt Lake City: Smith-Pettit Foundation, 2009), 3:1668.
29. Jeffrey R. Holland, "Lord, I Believe," *Ensign*, May 2013, 94.
30. Coventry Kersey Dighton Patmore, *The Rod, the Root, and the Flower* (London: George Bell, 1895), 194–95.
31. "History of Joseph Smith," *Millennial Star* 20.49 (4 December 1858): 774.
32. Dieter F. Uchtdorf, "Come, Join with Us," *Ensign*, November 2013, 23.

CHAPTER 9
THE TOO-TENDER HEART:
RETHINKING BEING "OVERCOME WITH EVIL"

1. Alfred, Lord Tennyson, "In Memoriam," LVII, in John D. Jump, ed., *In Memoriam, Maud, and Other Poems* (London: Dent and Sons, 1991), 103–4.
2. Nicholas Wolterstorff, *Lament for a Son* (Grand Rapids, Michigan: Eerdmans, 1987), 81.
3. C. S. Lewis, *Perelandra* (New York: Scribner, 1996), 142.
4. Norman Mailer, "Crucifying Mailer," *Toronto Star* (28 April 1997): E4.
5. Edward Beecher, *Concord of Ages: or The Individual and Organic Harmony of God and Man* (New York: Derby and Jackson, 1860), 98.
6. Romans 12:21.
7. Julian of Norwich, *Showings*, ed. Denise N. Baker (New York: Norton, 2005), XVI.76, p. 115.
8. Fyodor Dostoevsky, *The Brothers Karamazov* (New York: Penguin, 1978), 1:287–88.
9. Dostoevsky, *Brothers Karamazov*, 1:287.

10. Howard Schwartz, ed. *Gabriel's Palace: Jewish Mystical Tales* (New York: Oxford University Press, 1994), 267.
11. Wolterstorff, *Lament*, 80–81. Wolterstorff attributes the insight to an unnamed friend.
12. Mosiah 18:9.
13. Wolterstorff, *Lament*, 86.
14. Wolterstorff, *Lament*, 89.
15. Brigham Young, *Complete Discourses*, ed. Richard S. Van Wagoner (Salt Lake City: Smith-Pettit Foundation, 2009), 5:2540.
16. 1 Nephi 8:8–9.
17. Luke 2:25–38.
18. Mary Oliver, "Maybe," in *New and Selected Poems* (Boston: Beacon Press, 1993), 97–98.
19. Edmund Spenser, *The Faerie Queen*, V.ii.39.
20. Young, *Complete Discourses*, 5:3139.
21. D&C 6:22–23.
22. C. S. Lewis, *The Screwtape Letters: Annotated Edition* (New York: HarperCollins, 2013), 47–48.
23. Letter from Liberty Jail, Missouri, 25 March 1839, in Manuscript History of the Church (Church History Library), C-1, pp. 900–906, 907–12.
24. Quoted in *Mother Teresa, Come Be My Light: The Private Writings of the "Saint of Calcutta,"* ed. Brian Kolodiejchk (New York: Doubleday, 2007), 1–2.
25. Julian, *Showings*, XIV.41, p. 56.
26. Gerard Manley Hopkins, "I wake and feel," in *Poems* (New York: Oxford University Press, 1961), 109.
27. Deuteronomy 4:9.

CHAPTER 10

OF SILENCE AND SOLITUDE:
"SPEAK, LORD, FOR THY SERVANT HEARETH"

1. Siegfried Sassoon, "Alone," in *The Old Huntsman and Other Poems* (New York: Dutton, 1918), 89.
2. Percy B. Shelley, "Mont Blanc," in *The Lyric Poems of Shelley* (London: J. M. Dent, 1897), 162.
3. He wrote the poem "Surprised by Joy" to commemorate the painful moment of recollecting his "most grievous loss." In William Wordsworth, *Poetical Works* (Oxford: Oxford University Press, 1989), 204.
4. From his wife's memorial plaque, translation on display in the York Minster.
5. Gerard Manley Hopkins, "I wake and feel," in *Poems* (New York: Oxford University Press, 1961), 109.
6. *Mother Teresa, Come Be My Light: The Private Writings of the "Saint of Calcutta,"* ed. Brian Kolodiejchk (New York: Doubleday, 2007), 202.
7. "The Temple," *Times and Seasons* 3.13 (2 May 1842): 776.

8. "To William W. Phelps and Others," 18 August 1833, in Dean C. Jessee, ed., *Personal Writings of Joseph Smith*, rev. ed. (Salt Lake City: Deseret Book, 2002), 308–9.

9. "To Moses Nickerson," 19 November 1833, in Jessee, *Personal Writings*, 326.

10. "To Edward Partridge and Others," 10 December 1833, in Jessee, *Personal Writings*, 329.

11. See D&C 9.

12. "The Elders of the Church in Kirtland, to Their Brethren Abroad," 22 January 1834, in *Evening and Morning Star* 2.18 (March 1834): 142.

13. R. S. Thomas, "Nuclear," in *Collected Poems 1945–1990* (London: J. M. Dent, 1993), 317.

14. Marilynnne Robinson, *Gilead* (New York: Picador, 2004), 91.

15. Walker Percy, *The Second Coming* (New York: Picador, 1980), 360.

16. See M. Sue Bergin, *Am I a Saint Yet?* (Springville, UT: Cedar Fort, 2012), 65–66.

17. Russell Hancock, remarks transcribed by Geoff Nelson, "On Praying with Your Feet," *Dialogue* 45.4 (Winter 2012):173–74.

18. Philip Barlow, personal correspondence. He is citing David O. McKay in the phrase, "natural sequence . . ." See Clare Middlemiss, comp., *Cherished Experiences from the Writings of President David O. McKay* (Salt Lake City: Deseret Book, 1976), 6–7.

19. Franz Kafka, quoted in Andrew Vogel Ettin, *Betrayals of the Body Politic* (Charlottesville: University of Virginia Press, 1993), 95.

20. Luke 22:43.

Chapter 11
To the Godless and Guileless: Belief as Risk

1. George MacDonald, "December 31," in *Diary of an Old Soul* (Minneapolis: Augsburg, 1975), 132.

2. Robinson Jeffers, "The Epic Stars," in *The Selected Poetry of Robinson Jeffers* (Stanford: Stanford University Press, 2001), 699.

3. John D. Barrow and Frank J. Tippler, *The Anthropic Cosmological Principle* (Oxford: Oxford University Press, 2009), 2–5.

4. Martin Rees, *Just Six Numbers: The Deep Forces That Shape Our Universe* (New York: Basic Books, 2000), 99.

5. Richard Dawkins, *The God Delusion* (New York: Mariner Books, 2008), 162.

6. William Shakespeare, *Hamlet*, V.v.

7. Westminster Confession, Chapter III, Article I.

8. Interview with Terry Gross on "Fresh Air," http://www.npr.org/templates/story/story.php?storyId=9180871.

9. Stan Larson, "The King Follett Discourse: A Newly Amalgamated Text," *BYU Studies* 18.2 (Winter 1978): 201.

10. Dietrich Bonhöffer to Eberhard Bethge, 16 July 1944. In Larry L. Rasmussen,

Dietrich Bonhoeffer: Reality and Resistance (Louisville: Westminster John Knox Press, 2005), 17.

11. "The existence of mind is certainly a *datum* for the construction of any world picture: At the very least, its *possibility* must be explained. And it hardly seems credible that its appearance should be a natural accident, like the fact that there are mammals." (Thomas Nagel, *The Last Word* [New York: Oxford University Press, 1997], 132–33, 137–38). Dyson argues that theism must accommodate a robust human free will, and that consciousness cannot be reduced to chemical events (see Phillip F. Schewe, *Maverick Genius: The Pioneering Odyssey of Freeman Dyson* [New York: St. Martin's, 2013], 244–45).

12. See J. M. Ellis McTaggart, "Human Pre-Existence," *International Journal of Ethics* 15.1 (October 1904): 86–87.

13. See D&C 88:32; John 6:39.

14. Nathaniel Givens, "What It Would Take to Not Believe," *Times and Seasons* 14 April 2014, http://timesandseasons.org/index.php/2014/04/what-it-would-take-to-not-believe/.

15. See D&C 46:13–14.

16. See Jeffrey R. Holland, "Lord, I Believe," *Ensign*, May 2013, 93–95; Dieter F. Uchtdorf, "Come, Join with Us," *Ensign*, November 2013, 21–24.

17. George MacDonald, *Thomas Wingfold, Curate* (London: Hurst and Blackett, 1876), 3:65–66.

18. W. K. Clifford, "The Ethics of Belief," in *The Religious Experience*, ed. George Brantl (New York: George Braziller, 1964), 2:739.

19. William James, "The Will to Believe," in *The Will to Believe and Other Essays* (New York: Longmans, 1919), 18–19.

20. C. S. Lewis to Sister Penelope CSMV, 30 December 1950, in *Collected Letters*, ed. Walter Hooper (New York: HarperCollins, 2009), 3:79.

21. Milton Steinberg, *As a Driven Leaf* (n.p.: Behrman House, 1996), 243.

22. Thomas Carlyle, *On Heroes and Hero Worship* (London: Chapman and Hall, 1840), 4.

23. Alma 32:35.

24. Quoted in Stanley Hauerwas, *The Hauerwas Reader* (Durham, North Carolina: Duke University Press, 2001), 4.

Epilogue

Doubt and Discipleship

1. Thomas Traherne, "Life's Blessedness," in *Selected Poems* (Hull: J. R. Tutin, 1905), 3–24.

2. Flannery O'Connor, "To Louise Abbot," in *The Habit of Being: Letters of Flannery O'Connor*, ed. Sally Fitzgerald (New York: Farrar, Straus, Giroux, 1988), 353.

3. D&C 88:118; 109:7.

NOTES

4. Miguel de Unamuno, "Saint Manuel Bueno, Martyr," in *Ficciones*, trans. Anthony Kerrigan (Princeton: Princeton University Press, 1976), 7:176–77.
5. Alma 32:16.
6. C. S. Lewis to Sheldon Vanauken, 23 December 1950, in *Collected Letters*, ed. Walter Hooper (New York: HarperCollins, 2009), 3:75.
7. Nathaniel Hawthorne, *Mosses from an Old Manse* (Boston: Houghton Mifflin, 1882), 38.
8. Gerard Manley Hopkins, "As Kingfishers Catch Fire," in *Poems* (New York: Oxford University Press, 1948), 95.
9. Andrew F. Ehat and Lyndon W. Cook, eds., *The Words of Joseph Smith: The Contemporary Accounts of the Nauvoo Discourses of the Prophet Joseph Smith* (Orem, Utah: Grandin, 1994), 352.

INDEX

INDEX

INDEX

Talks, 42

Talmage, James E., W. E. Riter's letter to, 6–7

Taylor, John, 90–91

Temple ordinances, 46

Temple work, 68

Tennyson, Alfred, Lord, 109

Teresa, Mother, 118, 124

Theism, 160n11

Thinking, hero worship and, 63–64

Thirty-Nine Articles, 86–87

Thomas, R. S., 127

Traherne, Thomas, 89–90, 141–42

Trials, 79, 111–19, 144. *See also* Afflictions; Pain; Suffering

Trials of faith, 103–7, 113–14

Truth: openness to, 10; art and, 13–15; revealed through love, 16–18; Mormon monopoly on, 87–91

Uchtdorf, Dieter, 82

Unamuno, Miguel de, 143–44

Uncertainty, 34–36. *See also* Suspense

Voltaire, 36

Ward, Thomas, 90

Wards, community and, 43–44

War in heaven, 112–13

Wayward children, 94

Weaknesses, overcoming, 33

Wesley, John, 91

Wisdom, seeking, 99–102

Wolterstorff, Nicholas, 115

Woodruff, Wilford, 68, 92–93

Woolf, Virginia, 13

Woolley, Edwin D., 103

Wordsworth, William: on formation of self, 14; on immortality, 33–35; "Nuns Fret Not," 37; on rules, 48

Worldview, 2–10

Worship, 42–43

Young, Brigham: on self-governance, 33; on hero worship, 63; on Joseph Smith's weaknesses, 65; fallibility of, 69–70; on elect, 91; on salvation, 92, 93; on art, science, and literature, 101; tension between Edwin D. Woolley and, 103; on stereotyped Latter-day Saints, 104; on lacking joy, 115; on independence, 117

Zion, building, 102–3